The Economics of Public Issues

TWELFTH EDITION

Roger LeRoy Miller
Institute for University Studies
Arlington, Texas

Daniel K. Benjamin
Clemson University
and PERC, Bozeman, Montana

Douglass C. North
Washington University, St. Louis

Boston San Francisco New York
London Toronto Sydney Tokyo Singapore Madrid
Mexico City Munich Paris Cape Town Hong Kong Montreal

Executive Editor: Denise Clinton
Acquisitions Editor: Victoria Warneck
Developmental Editor: Rebecca Ferris
Editorial Assistant: Christine Houde
Managing Editor: James Rigney
Senior Production Supervisor: Nancy Fenton
Marketing Manager: Dara Lanier
Design Manager: Regina Hagen
Cover Designer: Anton Marc
Senior Manufacturing Buyer: Hugh Crawford
Composition and Prepress Services: Pre-Press Co., Inc.
Printer and Binder: R.R. Donnelley & Sons
Cover Photo: © PhotoDisc

Library of Congress Cataloging-in Publication Data

Miller, Roger LeRoy.
    The economics of public issues / Roger LeRoy Miller, Daniel K. Benjamin, Douglass C. North.— 12th ed.
        p.   cm.
    Includes bibliographical references and index.
    ISBN 0-321-07915-9 (pbk.)
        1. Economics. 2. Industrial policy. 3. Economic policy.
    I. Benjamin, Daniel K. II. North, Douglass Cecil. III. Title.

HB171 .M544 2001
330.973'092—dc21   00-035529

3 4 5 6 7 8 9 10—DOH—0 4 0 3 0 2 0 1

To Rod Kagan, whose sculptures keep getting better with age; thanks for your friendship.

R.L.M

To my students:
Noster patronis emptor est.

D.K.B.

Contents

Preface

This book is about some issues of our times. Several of these issues are usually thought of as being inherently non-economic. Others provide classic illustrations of the core of economic science. Many are controversial and thus are likely to evoke non-economic reactions to what we have to say. In our view, however, the one feature that ties all of the issues together is that they illustrate the power of economics in explaining the world around us. And, we might add, we hope all of them illustrate that economics can be entertaining as well as informative.

Over the years, we have sought to select issues for this book that—in addition to the attributes noted above—possess a sense of immediacy. We hope you will find the issues we have added for this edition meet this criterion. The new issues include the following:

- *Slave Redemption in Sudan*
- *Smoking and Smuggling*
- *Caught in Traffic*
- *The E-Commerce Explosion*
- *Pity the Poor Monopolist*
- *Killer Cars and the Rise of the SUV*
- *Superfund Follies*
- *The Economics of Weather Forecasting*
- *Property Rights and Forests*

All of the other chapters in this edition have been partially or completely rewritten, and every chapter is, of course, as up-to-date as we can make it. What you will consistently find is a straightforward application of economic principles as they are taught in virtually all courses in economics, public policy, and the social sciences. This book can be understood by those who have taken a course in economics, are taking a course in economics, or have never taken a course in economics. In other words, we have made it self-contained, as well as accessible to a wide range of students.

The chapters in this edition are organized into seven parts. Part One examines the foundations of all economic analysis, including the concepts of scarcity, trade-offs, opportunity cost, marginal analysis, and the like. In a sense, the four chapters in this introductory part set the stage for the remaining twenty-seven chapters. The second through sixth parts of the book cover the topics—such as demand and supply, market structures, environmental issues, and the impact of government policies—that are integral to virtually every course in which economics plays a role. At the end of the book, Part Seven examines the international scene, because international issues have become an essential part of the public issues of today.

Every part has a several-page introduction that prepares the reader for the material that is included in the following chapters. These part openers summarize and tie together the relevant issues, thus serving as launching pads for the analyses that follow. We hope you will have your students read these part openers before embarking on any of the chapters they precede.

Every instructor will want to order a copy of the *Instructor's Manual* that accompanies *The Economics of Public Issues*. In writing this manual we have tried to incorporate the very best of the teaching aids that we use when we teach from *The Economics of Public Issues*. For each chapter, the features of this manual are:

- A synopsis that cuts to the core of the economic issues involved in the chapter.
- A concise exposition of the "behind the scenes" economic analysis on which the discussion in the text is based. For almost all of the chapters, this exposition is supplemented with one or more diagrams that we have found to be particularly useful as teaching tools.
- Answers to the Discussion Questions posed at the end of the chapter—answers that further develop the basic economic analysis of the chapter, and almost always suggest new avenues of discussion.

The world of public issues continues to evolve. By the time you read this preface, we will be working on the next edition. If you have any particular subjects you would like to see included in the future, let us know by writing us in care of Addison Wesley Longman.

Several chapters in this edition draw on the "Tangents" column that Daniel K. Benjamin writes for *PERC Reports*. We are grateful to the Political Economy Research Center (PERC) for permission to use that material. In addition, literally dozens of kind users of the last edition of this book, as well as several extremely diligent and thoughtful reviewers, offered suggestions for the current edition. Although scarcity precluded us from adopting all of their recommendations, we believe the reviewers—James Bruehler (Eastern Illinois University), Kenny Christianson (Ithaca College), Richard Coffman (University of Idaho), Michael Davis (Southern Methodist University), Jan Gerson (University of Michigan), Tawni Hunt Ferrarini (Northern Michigan University), Dianne Long (California Polytechnic State University), James McBrearty (University of Arizona), Valerie Ramey (University of California, San Diego), and Allen Sanderson (University of Chicago)—will be able to identify the impact they each had on this edition. To them and to our users who wrote to us—especially Andy Herr's students at St. Vincent College—we offer our sincere thanks and hope that the end result was worthy of their time and concern. We also thank Rebecca Ferris for shepherding the project, and Robbie Benjamin, whose editorial skills once again have improved the final product. All errors remain, of course, solely our own.

R.L.M.

D.K.B.

D.C.N.

Part One

The Foundations of Economic Analysis

INTRODUCTION

Our world is one of **scarcity;** we want more than we have. The reason is simple. Although we live in a world of limited **resources,** we have unlimited wants. This does not mean we all live and breathe solely to drive the fastest cars or wear the latest clothes. It means that we all want the right to make decisions about how resources are used— even if what we want to do with those resources is to feed starving children in Third World nations.

Given the existence of scarcity, we must make choices; we cannot have more of everything, so to get more of some things, we must give up other things. Economists express this simple idea by saying that we face **trade-offs.** For example, a student who wants higher grades generally must devote more time to studying and less time to, say, going to the movies; the trade-off in this instance is between grades and entertainment.

The concept of a trade-off is one of the (surprisingly few) basic principles you must grasp to understand the economics of public issues. We illustrate the simplicity of these principles with Chapter 1, "Killer Airbags." It is possible you thought that the government mandated the use of automobile airbags to save people's lives. Indeed, that may well have been the motivation. But it turns out that airbags also kill some automobile occupants and induce drivers of airbag-equipped cars to drive in ways that endanger themselves and other persons. So, like many of the issues explored in this book, there is more to automobile safety—and government policy making—than meets the eye, but with the use of some simple economic principles, you can greatly expand both your vision and your understanding of them.

Chapter 2, "Terrible Trade-off," examines a behind-the-scenes trade-off made every day on our behalf by the U.S. Food and Drug Administration (FDA). This federal government agency is charged with ensuring that the new prescription medicines that reach the market are both safe and effective. In carrying out its duties, the FDA requires pharmaceutical companies to subject proposed new drugs to extensive testing before the drugs may be introduced to the market. When the FDA requires more exhaustive testing of a drug, this improves the chances that the drug will be both safe and effective. But additional testing slows the approval of new drugs, thus depriving some individuals of the ability to use the drugs to treat their illnesses. The drug approval process undoubtedly reduces pain and suffering for some people, and even saves the lives of others, because it reduces the chances that an unsafe or ineffective drug will reach the market. Yet because the process also reduces the rate at which drugs reach the market (and may even prevent some safe, effective drugs from ever being introduced), the pain and suffering of other individuals is increased. Indeed, some individuals die as a result. This, then, is the terrible trade-off we face in Chapter 2: Who shall live and who shall die?

If trade-offs, or choices, are present in all our activities, we must face the question of how we may make the best choices. Economists argue that doing so requires the use of what we call **marginal analysis:** The term *marginal* in this context means incremental, or additional. All choices involve costs and benefits—we give up something for anything that we get. As we engage in more of any activity (eating, studying, or sleeping, for example) the **marginal benefits** of that activity eventually decline: The *additional* benefits associated with an *additional* unit of the activity get lower. In contrast, the **marginal costs** of an activity eventually rise as we engage in more and more of it. The best choices are made when we equate the marginal benefits and marginal costs of activity; that is, we try to determine when engaging in any more of a given activity would produce additional costs in excess of the additional benefits.

In Chapter 3, "Flying the Friendly Skies?", we apply the principles of marginal analysis to the issue of airline safety. How safe is it to travel at 600 miles per hour 7 miles above the ground? How safe *should* it be? The answers to these and other questions can be explored using marginal analysis. One of the conclusions we reach is that *perfect* safety is simply not in the cards: Every time you step into an airplane (or even across the street) there is some risk that your journey will end unhappily. As disconcerting as this might sound at first, we think you will find after reading this chapter that once the costs and benefits are taken into account you would have it no other way.

Armed with the principles laid out in the first three chapters, we see in Chapter 4, "Choosing Crime," how they may be applied in yet another surprising venue: crime control. When politicians pat themselves on the back for how much they are spending on crime control, they are hoping you will ignore how much they are *not* spending; after all, as long as crime exists, there could be *less* crime. Of course, if we choose to have more crime control, we must have less of other things—trade-offs are present here, too. In the short run, having fewer burglaries may mean that we end up with more murders. In the long run, the trade-off may be that of accepting poorer schools in return for better law enforcement.

Chapter 4 also illustrates that the economic principles that are so powerful in understanding the operation of markets are also enlightening when applied to nonmarket settings, such as decision making by government agencies. Indeed, many governments are using the very economic principles we are discussing to make their agencies work more like private markets. We are led to conclude that in a world of scarcity, virtually every aspect of human behavior can be better understood through the application of the principles of economics.

1

Killer Airbags

Federal law requires that new cars be equipped with devices that kill drivers and passengers. If this sounds odd, the story gets stranger when you realize these devices are supposed to—and sometimes do—*save* lives. The devices in question are airbags, and their saga illustrates almost all of the important principles you should know to understand the economics of public issues.

The airbag story begins in 1969, when the Nixon Administration first proposed requiring "passive" restraints that would protect motorists during collisions even if they took no actions to protect themselves. The ideal system was thought to be airbags that would automatically inflate in the event of a collision. But a special government study commission found the airbags then available were not only extremely costly and unreliable but were in fact dangerous to the occupants of cars, especially to young children.[1] So, instead of airbags, the government tried requiring seat belts that prevented cars from being started unless the belts were fastened. Inconvenienced consumers who disliked seat belts quickly rejected these, and the idea of airbags was revived and eventually mandated by the federal government. In anticipation of the requirements that 1998 cars have them on both the driver and

---

[1] *Cumulative Regulatory Effects on the Cost of Automobile Transportation (RECAT): Final Report of the Ad Hoc Committee,* Office of Science and Technology, Washington, D.C., 1972.

passenger sides, carmakers began installing airbags on selected models in 1989. By 1997, more than 65 million cars had driver-side bags, and about 35 million had them on the passenger side, too. At first it seemed as though the earlier problems with airbags had been solved. The installed cost of about $400 apiece was far less than it would have been when the bags were initially proposed, and their reliability was dramatically increased. News reports soon began appearing with stories of seemingly miraculous survival by occupants of airbag-equipped cars in collisions. By the end of 1995, it was estimated that airbags had saved more than 1500 lives since 1989.

As the population of cars with airbags grew, however, another set of stories began to appear: Airbags deploy at speeds up to 200 mph and are designed to be most effective when used in conjunction with seat belts. It soon became apparent that people who failed to use belts, people who sat closer than the normal distance from the steering wheel or dashboard, and—most ominously—children anywhere in the front seat were at increased risk of serious injury or death due to airbag deployment. By late 1997 it was estimated that although a total (since 1989) of perhaps 2600 people owed their lives to airbags, there were more than 80 people, most of them children, who had been killed by the force of normally deploying airbags.

The outcry over the deaths of children killed in low-speed crashes by the very devices that were supposed to protect them generated action by both the private sector and the federal government. Auto manufacturers and their suppliers began developing "smart" airbags that sense the severity of a collision, the size of the person in the front seat, and whether the person is properly belted. Then, depending on the results of those measurements, the bag decides whether to deploy and at what speed it will do so. As an interim solution, in November 1997 (four and a half years after the first documented airbag fatality) the Department of Transportation announced that consumers would be allowed to apply for permission to have airbag cutoff switches installed in their vehicles. The estimated cost to consumers who have the switches installed is $150 to $200 per car.

Beginning with the 1998 model year, manufacturers also began installing less powerful airbags that inflate 22 percent less quickly on the driver side and 14 percent less quickly on the passenger side. The result has been a sharp reduction in (although not an elimination of) airbag-induced fatalities. By 2000, airbags had been credited with saving more than 4700 lives in serious, high-speed crashes since 1989, at a cost of about 150 children killed by airbag deployments in low-speed crashes.

What can we learn from the airbag episode that will guide us in thinking about other public issues of our times? There are several general principles:

1. *There is no free lunch.* Every choice, and thus every policy, entails a **cost**—something must be given up. In a world of scarcity, we cannot have more of everything, so to get more of some things, we must give up other things. Simply put, we face trade-offs. In this case, although airbags increase the safety of most adults, there is both a monetary cost of $800 per car and a reduced level of safety for children riding in the front seat.

2. *The cost of an action is the alternative that is sacrificed.* Economists often express costs (and benefits) in terms of dollars, because this is a simple means of accounting for and measuring them. But that doesn't mean costs have to be monetary, nor does it mean economics is incapable of analyzing costs and benefits that are very human. In the case of airbags, the cost that induced action by consumers, manufacturers, and government officials was the lost lives of scores of children.

3. *The relevant costs and benefits are the marginal (or incremental) ones.* The relevant question is not whether safety is good or bad; it is instead how much safety we want—which can only be answered by looking at the added (or marginal) benefits of more safety compared to the added (marginal) costs. One possible response to the child fatalities would have been to outlaw airbags on new cars and mandate that all installed airbags be deactivated. That would have guaranteed that no more children would have been killed by airbags. But for many people (such as those without young children), this solution to airbag fatalities would not be sensible, because the marginal cost would exceed the marginal benefit.

4. *People respond to incentives.* A rise in the apparent costs of using airbags (due to airbag fatalities among children) reduced consumers' desire to utilize airbags and induced them to put pres-

sure on the federal government—pressure that convinced the Department of Transportation to change the regulations. Moreover, the simultaneous rise in the rewards of developing alternatives to today's airbags sent suppliers scurrying to find those alternatives, including "smart" airbags.

5. *Policies always have unintended consequences, and as a result, their net benefits are almost always less than anticipated.* Information, like all goods, is costly to obtain, and sometimes the cheapest way to learn more about something is simply to try it. When it is tried, new things will be learned, not all of them pleasant. More importantly, in the case of government regulations, Principle 3 (above) fails to make good headlines. Instead, what gets politicians reelected and regulators promoted are fundamental, *absolute* notions, such as "safety" (and motherhood and apple pie). Thus, if a little safety is good, more must be better, so why not simply mandate that all front-seat passengers in all cars be protected by airbags that are all the same? Eventually, the reality of Principle 3 sinks in, but in this case not before scores of children had lost their lives.

Although these basic principles of public issues are readily apparent when looking at the children who have been killed by airbags, they are just as present in two other features of airbags—neither of which has received much attention. First, most airbag deployments occur in relatively low-speed accidents (under 30 miles per hour), when the added safety benefits to properly belted occupants is low. But once the bags are deployed, they must be replaced, and often so must the windshield (blown out by the passenger-side bag) and sometimes even the dashboard (damaged as the airbag deploys). The added repair cost per car is currently estimated to be between $2000 and $2500. Thus, not only are automobile repair costs soaring due to airbags, many cars that routinely would have been repaired are now being written off completely because it is too costly to fix them.

Second, and more significantly, cars that are airbag-equipped tend to be driven more aggressively, apparently because their occupants feel more secure. The result is more accidents by such cars, more serious accidents (such as rollovers) that kill occupants despite the airbags, and a higher risk of pedestrian fatalities—none of which are accounted for in the lives-saved figures that we quoted earlier.[2] In addition, when seat belts are worn, they are almost as good as airbags in preventing fatalities among automobile occupants. Belts reduce the fatality rate by 45 percent; adding an airbag increases this only to 50 percent. The net effect is that even though airbags are both better and less costly than they were when first proposed, it is still not clear they yield benefits that exceed their costs.

DISCUSSION QUESTIONS

1. Under what circumstances is it appropriate to trade off human lives against dollars when making decisions about safety?

2. Do you think government action allowing airbag deactivation would have been as swift or as likely if all the fatalities had been among adults rather than chiefly among small children? (Some of the airbag-induced fatalities were petite women who were sitting closer to the steering wheel than allowed for in the design calculations done on the basis of the seating behavior of the average male.)

3. Given estimates that 2600 lives had been saved by airbags, why did it take only 80 airbag-induced fatalities (rather than, say, 2600) to get the government to change the regulations?

4. Most people—and without any government regulation requiring it—have locks on their doors to protect them from intruders. If airbags are so good at protecting people from injuries and death, why were government regulations required to get them installed on automobiles?

[2] Steven Peterson, George Hoffer, and Edward Millner, "Are Drivers of Air-Bag-Equipped Cars More Aggressive? A Test of the Offsetting Behavior Hypothesis," *The Journal of Law & Economics,* October, 1995, pp. 251–264.

2

Terrible Trade-off

How would you rather die? Due to a lethal reaction to a drug prescribed by your doctor? Or because your doctor failed to prescribe a drug that would have saved your life? If this choice is one you would rather not make, consider this: Employees of the United States Food and Drug Administration (FDA) make that decision on behalf of millions of Americans many times each year. More precisely, the FDA decides whether new medicines (prescription drugs) should be allowed to go on sale in the United States. If the FDA decides to allow a drug to be sold, doctors may prescribe it, in the expectation that the beneficial effects of the drug will outweigh whatever adverse side effects the drug may have. But if the FDA prohibits the drug from being sold in the United States, doctors here may not legally prescribe it, even if thousands of lives are saved by the drug each year in other countries.

The FDA's authority to make such decisions dates back to the passage of the Food and Drug Safety Act of 1906. That law required, among other things, that medicines be correctly labeled as to their contents and that they not contain any substances poisonous or harmful to the health of consumers. Because of this legislation, Dr. Hostatter's celebrated Stomach Bitters and Kickapoo Indian Sagwa, along with numerous rum-laden concoctions, cocaine-based potions, and supposed anticancer remedies, disappeared from druggists' shelves. The law was expanded in 1938 with the passage of the federal Food, Drug, and Cosmetic Act, which forced manufacturers to demonstrate the safety of new drugs before being allowed to offer them for sale. (This legislation was driven by the deaths of 107 individuals who had taken an elixir of sulfanilamide, which happened to contain diethylene glycol, a poisonous substance usually contained in antifreeze.)

The next step in U.S. drug regulation came after the birth of 12,000 deformed infants whose mothers during pregnancy had taken a sleeping pill called thalidomide. When these deformities first became apparent, the drug already was widely used in Europe, and the FDA was moving toward approving it in the United States. In fact, about 2.5 million thalidomide tablets were in the hands of U.S. physicians as samples. The FDA ordered all the samples removed and prohibited the sale of thalidomide in the United States. Using this incident as ammunition, Senator Estes Kefauver secured passage of a bill known as the 1962 Kefauver–Harris Amendments to the 1938 Food, Drug, and Cosmetic Act. This legislation radically altered the drug approval process in the United States.

Prior to the 1962 amendments, the FDA usually approved a new drug application within a 180-day time limit, unless the application failed to demonstrate that the drug was safe for use in the proposed manner. The 1962 amendments added a "proof of efficacy" requirement and also removed the time constraint on the FDA. Thus, since 1962, manufacturers wishing to introduce a new drug must demonstrate to the FDA's satisfaction that the drug is safe to use in the proposed manner, and also that it will accomplish the intended therapeutic outcome. Moreover, the FDA is free to determine how much and what evidence it will demand before approving a drug for sale, and it may take as long as it wants before either giving or refusing approval.

The most noticeable impact of the 1962 amendments was a reduction in the number of new drugs coming onto the market. Researchers have estimated that the 1962 amendments cut new drug introductions by as much as two-thirds. This occurred because the amendments sharply increased the costs of introducing a new drug and markedly slowed the approval process. Prior to the 1962 amendments, for example, the average time between filing and approval of a new drug application was seven months; by 1967, it was 30 months; and by the late 1970s, it had risen to eight to ten *years*. Although the average approval time has since dropped, it still takes nearly ten times as long for a new drug to be approved as it did before the 1962 amendments. The protracted approval process involves costly testing by the drug companies and delays the receipt of any potential revenue from new drugs. Moreover, once all of the test data is in, the FDA may decide against the company's application. Overall, the expected profitability of new drugs has been reduced by the 1962 amendments, so fewer of them have been brought onto the market.

The rationale behind the FDA regulations is presumably protection of consumers, because generally consumers do not have the ability to obtain or analyze the information necessary to make accurate choices about the safety or efficacy of particular drugs. Consumers are at the mercy of the physicians who prescribe the drugs. But the physicians are also, in a sense, at the mercy of the drug companies, for it is almost impossible for each individual doctor to keep up with all of the technical literature about drugs and be aware of the advantages and disadvantages of each of them. Doctors must rely on the so-called detail people sent out by the drug companies to inform physicians about new drugs and give them samples to dispense to their patients, so that doctors can see for themselves how effective the new drugs really are. Without FDA regulations, it is argued, the drug companies might introduce drugs that are not completely safe or simply do not work as well as they might.

Countering this argument is that doctors, hospitals, and drug companies have strong incentives to prescribe, market, and produce drugs that are both safe and effective. After all, if it can be proven that side effects from a drug cause harm to an individual, or that an individual was harmed because a drug did not perform as promised, the ensuing lawsuit can cost the doctor, hospital, or manufacturer millions of dollars. Moreover, doctors, hospitals, and drug companies rely heavily on their reputations, and serious errors in prescribing, marketing, or producing drugs can damage those reputations beyond repair.

Although debate remains over exactly how much regulation is needed to ensure that drugs are both safe and efficacious, there is little doubt that the 1962 amendments have resulted in a U.S. "drug lag." The number of drugs marketed in the United Kingdom that are not available in the United States, for example, is very much larger than the number marketed in the United States that are not available in the United Kingdom. Although the FDA and its supporters note that it takes time to ensure that patients benefit from rather than are harmed by new drugs, regulation-induced drug lag can *itself* be life-threatening. Dr. George Hitchings, a winner of the Nobel Prize in Medicine, has estimated that the five-year lag in introducing Septra (an antibacterial agent) to the United States "killed 100,000, maybe a million people" in this country. Similarly, the introduction of a class of drugs called beta blockers (used to treat heart attack victims and people with high blood pressure) was delayed nearly a decade in this country relative to its introduction in Europe. According to several researchers, the lag in the FDA approval of these drugs cost the lives of at least 250,000 Americans.

Now we can see the terrible trade-off in the market for prescription drugs: Although lives are saved because unsafe or ineffective drugs are kept off the market, the FDA regulatory process delays (or even prevents) the introduction of some safe and efficacious drugs, thereby costing lives. If the only cost of FDA-mandated testing were the millions of dollars that drug companies must spend on those procedures, there probably would not be many critics of the FDA. But the fact is that many persons could have benefited greatly—perhaps to the extent of being alive today—had the 1962 Kefauver–Harris Amendments not delayed the introduction of so many drugs.

With this thought in mind, let us take a more systematic look at the trade-off we face. Every time a new drug is introduced, there is a chance that it should not have been—either because it has adverse side effects that outweigh the therapeutic benefits (it is not safe), or because it really does nothing significant to help the individuals who take it (it is not effective). When such a drug is introduced, we shall say that a **Type I error** has been committed. Since 1962, incidence of Type I error—the thalidomide possibility—has been reduced by increasing the amount of prior testing for new drugs. People have surely benefited from this reduction in Type I error by incurring fewer adverse side effects and by being spared the costs of taking ineffective drugs. But other people have been the victims of what is called **Type II error.** Their cost is the pain, suffering, and death that occur because the 1962 amendments have prevented or delayed the introduction of safe, efficacious drugs. Type II error occurs when a drug *should* be introduced but is not, because of FDA regulation.

Does the apparently high incidence of Type II errors by the FDA over the past 40 years imply that the regulatory process should

be overhauled radically? Possibly, but even doing so would not eliminate the fundamental trade-off. The FDA's long, intensive review of
new drug applications does produce benefits: The drugs that eventually reach the market are safer and more effective. As we have seen,
the costs are that some safe, effective drugs never make it to the
market, and many others are substantially delayed. Expediting the
review process would enable more drugs to reach the market
sooner, but it would also increase the chances that a harmful or ineffective drug might slip through the screening process.

It seems that for every benefit there is a cost. Indeed, this simple fact is so pervasive in our lives that economists have even
coined a phrase summarizing it—*There is no such thing as a free
lunch*—which simply means that in a world of scarcity, every
choice we make entails a cost. By choosing to reduce the risk of introducing another thalidomide, we also choose to increase the risk
of delaying another Septra or beta blocker. Trade-offs such as this
are an inescapable fact.

The principles involved in making the best choices among
trade-offs are discussed in Chapter 1. On the drug front, outcries
over the high incidence of Type II errors by the FDA have in some
cases induced the agency to shorten the testing period for drugs
when the costs of Type I error are insignificant compared to the possible damage due to Type II error—as is the case with terminally ill
patients. Thus, since the 1980s, the FDA has accelerated the approval process for several drugs used in treating patients with
terminal diseases. One of the most famous of these drugs is azi-
dothymidine (AZT), which emerged in 1986 as a possible treatment
for AIDS. AZT received FDA approval after a testing period of
only 18 months when it was found that the drug increased the life
expectancy of AIDS patients. In effect, the FDA decided that the
costs associated with Type I error—such as headaches and nausea—
were outweighed by the many deaths that would result if the drug
were not approved quickly.

Despite the expedited review of AZT and a number of other
drugs used to treat AIDS or cancer, most of the agency's critics remain convinced that the FDA has too often weighed the terrible
trade-off of drug regulation in a way that has produced tragedy for
patients. As the battle against AIDS continues, there is little doubt
that pressure on the FDA to expedite the drug review process will

increase. Only time and careful scrutiny will enable us to determine whether future choices by the FDA help us or harm us.

DISCUSSION QUESTIONS

1. Does the structure of the drug industry have any bearing on the types of errors that drug firms are likely to make? That is, would a drug industry comprised of numerous highly competitive firms be more or less likely to introduce unsafe drugs than would an industry comprised of a few large firms?

2. How could the incentives facing officials at the FDA be changed to reduce the incidence of Type II errors?

3. What would be the advantages and disadvantages of a system in which, rather than having the FDA permit or prohibit new drugs, the FDA merely published its opinions about the safety and efficacy of drugs, and then allowed physicians to make their own decisions about whether to prescribe them for their patients?

4. Suppose, for simplicity, that Type I and Type II errors resulted in deaths only. Keeping in mind that too little caution produces Type I errors and too much caution produces Type II errors, what would be the best mix of Type I and Type II errors?

3

Flying the Friendly Skies?

Most of us hop into our cars with little thought for our personal safety beyond, perhaps, the act of putting on seat belts. Yet even though travel on scheduled, commercial airlines is far safer than driving to work or to the grocery store, many people approach air travel with a sense of foreboding, if not downright fear.

If we were to think carefully about the wisdom of traveling 600 miles per hour in an aluminum tube seven miles above the earth, several questions might come to mind: How safe is this? How safe should it be? Since the people who operate airlines are not in it for fun, does their interest in making a buck ignore our interest in making it home in one piece? Is government regulation the only way to ensure safety in the skies?

The science of economics begins with one simple principle: We live in a world of scarcity. As a result, to get more of any good, we must make some sacrifice of other goods. This is just as true of safety as it is of pizzas or haircuts or works of art. Safety confers benefits (we live longer and more enjoyably), but achieving it also entails costs (we must give up something to obtain that safety).

As the degree of safety rises, the total benefits of safety rise but the marginal (or incremental) benefits of additional safety decline. Consider a simple example: Having four exit doors on an airplane instead of three increases the number of people who can escape in the event of an emergency evacuation. Similarly, having five doors rather than four would enable still more people to evacuate safely. In both cases, more doors mean more people evacuated without injury, so the total benefits from safety rise with the number of doors. Nevertheless, the fifth door adds less in safety benefits than does the fourth door; if the fourth enables, say, an extra ten people to escape, the fifth may enable only an extra six to escape. (If this sounds implausible, imagine having a door for each person; the last door added will enable at most one more person to escape.) So we say that the marginal (or incremental) benefit of safety declines as the amount of safety increases.

Let's look now at the other side of the equation: As the amount of safety increases, both the total and the marginal (or incremental) costs of providing safety rise. Having a fuel gauge on the plane's instrument panel clearly enhances safety, because it reduces the chance that the plane will run out of fuel while in flight.[1] It is always possible that a fuel gauge will malfunction, so having a backup fuel gauge also adds to safety. Because having two gauges is more costly than having just one, the total costs of safety rise as safety increases. It is also clear, however, that although the cost of the second gauge is (at least) as great as the cost of the first, the second gauge has a smaller positive impact on safety. Thus, the cost per unit of additional (or incremental) safety is higher for the second fuel gauge than for the first.

How much safety should we have? For an economist, the answer to such a question is generally expressed in terms of marginal benefits and marginal costs. The economically efficient level of safety occurs when the marginal costs of safety equal the marginal benefits of that safety. Consider the example of doors on an airplane. Suppose that having a fourth door confers $1 million in benefits, whereas the cost of adding the door amounts to only $300,000. The net benefit of having the door is $700,000, and, from an economic standpoint, it is efficient to have the fourth door. Contrast this with the prospect of having thirteen doors on an airplane. Suppose that the thirteenth door confers benefits of $150,000 but that the cost of adding the thirteenth door is $900,000. In this case, the additional benefits of the door are less than the additional costs. Adding the door costs more than it is worth, so the door should not be added.

---

[1] Notice that we say "reduces" rather than "eliminates." In 1978 a United Airlines pilot preoccupied with a malfunctioning landing gear evidently failed to pay sufficient attention to his cockpit gauges. Eight people were killed when the plane was forced to crash land after running out of fuel.

In general, the efficient level of safety will not be perfect safety, because perfection is simply too costly to achieve. For example, to be absolutely *certain* that no one is ever killed or injured in an airplane crash, we would have to prevent all travel in airplanes. This does not mean that it is efficient to have airplanes dropping out of the sky like autumn leaves. It does mean that it is efficient for there to be *some* risk associated with air travel. The unavoidable conclusion is that if we wish to enjoy the advantages of flying, we must be willing to accept some risk—a conclusion that each of us implicitly accepts every time we step aboard an airplane.

Changes in circumstances can alter the efficient level of safety. For example, if a technological change reduces the costs of manufacturing and installing airplane doors, the marginal costs of providing a safe means of exit will be lower. Hence, it will be efficient to have more doors installed, implying that air travel will become safer. Similarly, if the marginal benefits of safety rise for some reason—perhaps because the president of the United States is on board—it could be efficient to take more precautions, resulting in safer air travel. Given the factors that determine the benefits and costs of safety, the result of a change in circumstances will be some determinate level of safety that generally will imply some risk of death or injury.

Do airlines in fact provide the efficient level of safety? If information were free, the answer to this question would have to be "yes." Consumers would simply observe the levels of safety provided by different airlines and the prices they charge, and select the degrees of safety that best suited their preferences and budgets—just as with other goods. But, of course, information is not free; it is a **scarce good,** costly to obtain. As a result, it is possible that passengers are unaware of the safety records of various airlines, just as they may be unaware of the competency of pilots and the maintenance procedures of an airline's mechanics. The fact that information about safety is not free has been used to argue that it is appropriate for the federal government to mandate certain minimum levels of safety, as it does today through the operation of the Federal Aviation Administration (FAA).

The argument in favor of government safety standards rests on the presumption that, left to their own devices, airlines would provide less safety than passengers actually want to have. This might happen, for example, if customers could not tell (at a reasonable cost) whether the equipment, training, procedures, and so on employed by an airline are safe. For example, how many airline passengers are experts in metal fatigue or are knowledgeable about the amount of training required to pilot a 747? If passengers cannot cheaply gauge the level of safety, they will not be willing or able to reward airlines for being safe or punish them for being unsafe. Consider a simple analogy: How much would you pay for a new set of clothes if the clothes were invisible? Not much, we would guess, unless you were an egotistical emperor. Hence, the reasoning goes, safety is costly to provide and consumers are unwilling to pay for it because they cannot accurately measure it; thus airlines provide too little of it. The conclusion, at least as reached by some, is that we should have a body of government experts—such as the FAA—set safety standards for the industry.

This conclusion seems plausible, but it ignores two simple points. First, how is the government to know what the efficient level of safety is? Assume for the moment that the FAA employs persons who are experts in metal fatigue, pilot training, maintenance procedures, and so on. Assume also that the FAA knows (1) the impact of these matters on the likelihood of deaths and injuries due to plane crashes and (2) exactly how much it costs to implement various safety improvements.[2] The FAA still does not have enough information to set efficient safety standards because it does not know the value that people place on safety. Without such information, the FAA has no way of assessing the benefits of additional safety and thus no means of knowing whether those benefits are greater or less than the costs.[3]

The second point is perhaps more fundamental. It is likely that people are really interested in reaching their destinations safely and not in whether they got there because of a good plane, a good pilot, or a good mechanic. Even if they cannot observe if an airline hires good pilots or bad pilots, they can observe whether that airline's

---

[2] Many people would argue that these assumptions presume that the FAA knows more than it could possibly know; we make the assumptions only to present the case for government safety regulations in the best light.

[3] Even if FAA experts know how much *they* benefit from additional safety, how are they to know how much *you* benefit?

planes land safely or crash—if for no other reason than because airplane crashes are the subject of intense media scrutiny. If it is *safety* that is important to consumers—and not the obscure, costly-to-measure set of reasons for that safety—the fact that consumers cannot easily measure metal fatigue in jet engines may be totally irrelevant to the process of achieving the efficient level of safety. If you know that an airline's planes have a nasty habit of hitting mountains, do you really care whether it is because their pilots have bad eyesight or because their planes have no altimeters?

Interestingly, evidence shows that consumers *are* cognizant of the safety performance of airlines, and that they punish airlines that perform in an unsafe manner. Researchers have found that when an airline is at fault in a fatal plane crash, consumers appear to downgrade their safety rating of the airline (i.e., revise upward their estimates of the likelihood of future fatal crashes).[4] As a result, the offending airline suffers substantial, adverse financial consequences, over and above the costs of losing the plane and being sued on behalf of the victims. Although these research findings do not guarantee that airlines provide the efficient level of safety, they do reveal that the market punishes unsafe performance—suggesting a striking degree of safety awareness on the part of supposedly ignorant consumers. If consumers (who are, after all, the ultimate judges of the value of their own safety) can accurately and cheaply judge the outcomes of the safety procedures followed by airlines, ignorance about the nature of those procedures may be irrelevant to the provision of the efficient level of safety.

We began this chapter by repeating the commonplace observation that airlines are safer than cars. Yet many people *still* worry for their safety every time they get on an airplane. Are they being irrational? Well, the answer, it seems, is in the eye of the beholder. Measured in terms of fatalities per mile traveled, airplanes are indeed some 15 times safer than cars (and 176 times safer than walking, we might add). But this number masks the fact that 68 percent of aircraft accidents happen on takeoff and landing, and these operations occupy only 6 percent of flight time. When the safety figures are recalculated on the basis of fatalities per *trip*, cars are

---

[4] Mark L. Mitchell and Michael T. Maloney, "Crisis in the Cockpit? The Role of Market Forces in Promoting Air Travel Safety," *Journal of Law & Economics*, October 1989, pp. 139–184.

actually 12 times safer than airplanes! And even if we look at perhaps the most neutral measure of safety—fatalities per person-hour traveled—it turns out that cars and planes are about equally safe. So, pick whatever measure of safety seems appropriate to you, but whatever mode of travel you use, we suggest: Buckle up.

DISCUSSION QUESTIONS

1. Is it possible to be too safe? Explain what you mean by "too safe."

2. Many automobile manufacturers routinely advertise the safety of their cars, yet airlines generally do not even mention safety in their advertising. Can you suggest an explanation for this difference?

3. Many economists would argue that private companies are likely to be more efficient than the government in operating airlines. Yet many economists would also argue that there is a valid reason for government to regulate the safety of those same airlines. Can you explain why (or why not) the government might be good at ensuring safety, even though it might not be good at operating the airlines?

4. Professional football teams sometimes charter airplanes to take them to their away games. Would you feel safer riding on a United Airlines plane that had been chartered by the Washington Redskins rather than on a regularly scheduled United Airlines flight?

4

Choosing Crime

How much is crime prevention worth? Plenty, apparently—at least in New York City, which spends over $3 *billion* a year on its police department. That works out to about $400 a year for each of the city's residents, or $1600 for a family of four. Why do New Yorkers spend so much on crime prevention? If the answer seems obvious, then why don't they spend even *more*? (After all, hundreds of murders are committed in New York City each year, and many residents there consider muggings and burglaries as much a part of life as rude taxi drivers.) Would spending more on the police department reduce crime in New York City? If it would, then why did the city council decide to *permit* so much crime—by spending only $3 billion? If such spending does not deter crime, why isn't the police department simply abolished, with the savings used to improve the city's decaying school system?

Before we can begin to answer these questions, we must look at the economics of fighting crime. First of all, it is not just the police that are involved in crime prevention. The courts and the prison system also enter the picture, as do devices such as burglar alarms, locks, and safes. Second, we start with the presumption that spending more on crime prevention makes it more difficult (costly) for people to commit crimes and for them to avoid detection and punishment. Thus, devoting more resources to law enforcement will, to some degree, deter crime.

The costs of law enforcement can be divided into three general areas. First, there are the costs of crime detection and the arrest of suspects. Second, costs are incurred in the trial and conviction of the prisoner; they vary with the efficiency and speed with which the law enforcement officials and the courts can act. Third, once a sentence is imposed, there are the economic costs of maintaining and staffing prisons. (This third area, as well as the effectiveness of various deterrents to crime, are examined in Chapter 21.)

Even though an increase in the resources devoted to discovering and apprehending criminals can be expected to reduce crime, the optimum allocation of those resources is not so clear-cut. The chief of police or commissioner is faced with two sets of problems. He or she must decide how to divide the funds between capital and labor; that is, whether to choose more cars, equipment, and laboratories or more patrol officers, detectives, and technicians. The chief must also allocate funds among the various police details within the department; that is, decide whether to clamp down harder on homicide, car theft, or drug traffic.

Within a law enforcement budget of a given size, the police chief must therefore determine the optimum combination of production factors. The ideal combination is one in which an additional dollar spent on any input will provide an equal additional amount of crime prevention. If an additional dollar spent on laboratory equipment would yield a higher crime-deterrent result than if the dollar were spent on a police officer's salary, the laboratory would win. Clearly, this decision may change with changes in relative prices. For example, if the salaries of police officers increase, the balance may tip toward the use of more cars or equipment, depending on how well capital can be substituted for labor in a given situation. Instead of using two police officers in a car, it might be efficient to equip the car with bulletproof glass and let the driver patrol alone.

The police chief must also determine how to allocate resources among the interdepartmental details. Sometimes highly publicized events influence this decision. For example, several years ago prostitution increased in downtown Seattle, leading local merchants to complain that streetwalkers were hurting business. The merchants induced the police chief to increase sharply the detection and apprehension of prostitutes. That meant using more personnel and equipment on the vice squad; within a fixed budget, this could be done only by pulling resources away from homicide, robbery, and other details. In effect, the cost of reducing prostitution was an increase in assault and robbery.

The second area of law enforcement that incurs costs is the trial and its outcome. Recent studies indicate that the likelihood of conviction is a highly important factor in the prevention of crime. Currently, the probability of conviction and punishment for crime is extremely low in the United States. Nationwide, the odds of imprisonment for committing a crime are less than 1 in 20. In New York City, it has been estimated that an individual who commits a felony faces only a 1 in 200 chance of going to jail. Poor crime detection partly explains such incredible figures; court congestion adds to the problem. In big cities, the court calendar is so clogged that the delay in getting a case to trial may stretch from months into years.[1] Many observers believe that society is underinvesting in the resources needed to improve this process. If more were spent on streamlining court proceedings instead of on making arrests, cases could be brought to trial more promptly, the presence of all witnesses could be more easily secured, and the district attorney would not be forced to plea bargain with suspects. Faced with the probability of a quick and efficient trial, a potential criminal might think harder about robbing a bank or mugging a pedestrian.

We can now return to our original question. How did New York City determine that a budget of $3 billion for crime prevention was the right amount? In the short run, the city was faced with a total budget of a given size and had to decide how to carve it up between law enforcement and other municipal demands, such as fire protection, health, parks, streets, and libraries. Presumably, the mayor and the city council attempt to choose a combination of spending on all agencies that will yield an amount of public services with the greatest value. If additional money spent on fire protection does not yield as much "good" as it would if spent on police protection, then the amount should be allocated to law enforcement.

The short-run constraint of a fixed budget for law enforcement may be altered in the long run by asking the state legislature for increased funds for crime prevention. The legislature will then have to wrestle with the same allocation problem that engaged the city council: Will spending an additional dollar on higher education yield greater returns for society than the same dollar directed to crime prevention?

---

[1] Many court calendars are solidly booked for several years into the future. In New York City, for example, the average time lapse between filing a civil suit and getting it to trial is nearly three and a half *years.*

If the state chooses to raise taxes, this will broaden the allocation problem. The increased taxes will reduce the disposable income of some part of the citizenry. Those who pay the additional taxes must decide whether the additional public services are worthwhile. If they do not think so, at the next election they may vote to "throw the bums out."

Our description suggests that nonmarket solutions to economic problems parallel market solutions. Although we have focused on crime prevention, the criteria are similar for all types of government decisions and for all levels of government—local, state, and federal. Nevertheless, certain differences must be noted between decision making in the private, market sector of the economy and in the public, nonmarket sector. Problems of measurement are much greater in the latter. How, for example, do we put a price tag on recreation, which is the output of the parks department? The signals come through much louder and more clearly in market situations, in which changes in private profitability directly indicate which policies will be best. Instead of market signals, makers of public policy receive a confused set of noises generated by opponents and proponents of their decisions. A legislator is in the unenviable position of trying to please constituents while operating with very incomplete information.

Some cities have tried to use market mechanisms to improve crime prevention. A few years ago, the city of Orange, California, near Los Angeles, started paying its police according to how much crime was reduced. The incentive scheme applied to four categories of crime—burglary, robbery, rape, and auto theft. Under the plan, as first put into effect, if the crime rate in those categories was cut by a certain amount during the previous year, the police would get an extra 1 percent raise. If the crime rate was cut even more, the pay increase would be an extra 2 percent. The results were encouraging. Detectives on their own time produced videotape briefings with leads for patrol officers on specific beats. The whole force developed a campaign to encourage safety precautions in residents' homes. Statistically speaking, the results were even more impressive, for during the initial phase of the program crime in the four target categories fell by almost *triple* the most optimistic goal. The other crime figures held steady, indicating that the police force was not merely shifting its efforts from one area of crime to another.

Let us consider a closely related matter. What if a city or a state were responsible for restitution of the full cost of a crime committed within its borders? One might guess that unlimited liability on the part of government for crimes against the populace would certainly alter the present allocation of resources between crime prevention and other public endeavors.

Such liability would raise another problem. If victims of robberies, for example, were fully compensated by the municipality, there would be less incentive for individuals to protect themselves privately against robberies. The same is true for other crimes. One way to avoid this so-called *moral hazard* would be to establish a deductible on the municipality's liability. For example, for home robberies, the municipality might be held responsible for all losses in excess of $500. If this were the case, homeowners still would have an incentive to lock their doors, have watchdogs, and keep lights on at night when they are away.

Another way in which the allocation of crime prevention resources might be altered is demonstrated by a pilot project in crime prevention in Newport News, Virginia, a Navy port city with a population of about 180,000. Aided by a $1.2 million grant from the federal government, the police sought to deter crime before the fact rather than punishing it after the fact. At the heart of the program was a crime analysis model, a lengthy questionnaire filled out by police officers whenever a crime was committed. Analysis of these reports over time enabled the police to predict, with a surprising degree of accuracy, where crimes were likely to be committed. Steps could then be taken to prevent the crime by drawing on other public and private resources, such as community health clinics, social workers, attorneys, and welfare agencies. By analyzing homicide cases over an eighteen-month period, for example, the police found that 50 percent of all the murders committed had involved family members of the victims and that in half of those cases the police had already received complaints of domestic violence. As a result, a new procedure was implemented. Police began making arrests whenever they witnessed domestic violence, without waiting for a family member to swear out a warrant. The arrested party was placed in jail and released only if the individual agreed to professional counseling. The program seemed to work: For the five years preceding the experiment, the city had averaged twenty-five murders per year—half of them the result of domestic violence. During the pilot program, the murder rate was cut by two-thirds, and domestic murders were reduced even more. In all areas of crime—prostitution, robberies, burglaries, and nuisance crimes such as petty theft and vandalism—similar prevention techniques have been used successfully.

Traditionally, police have responded to crime, rather than taking an active preventive role. The Newport News program involves a radical reorientation of the work of the police. The results of the experiment suggest that perhaps, if more money and resources were allocated to crime prevention before the fact, the high cost of crime might be reduced for victims and taxpayers alike. Crime costs. So does crime prevention. But the latter has benefits to society that should be weighed when making decisions about law enforcement methods and expenditures.

DISCUSSION QUESTIONS

1. Discuss the allocation of resources for nonmarket activities such as higher education, firefighting, and highway construction.

2. How does a private firm decide how to allocate resources? How does the decision-making process differ from that of a government agency?

3. Large cities generally spend more per capita on crime prevention than do small towns. Economists would suggest that this difference is due to differences in both the costs and benefits of (1) committing crimes and (2) preventing crimes in large cities compared to small towns. Can you suggest what some of these differences in costs and benefits might be?

4. Economists speak of economic agents (such as the chief of police in this chapter) making decisions as though they wish to maximize the net benefits of their decisions. Do individuals have to think in the same terms that economists do for our *theories* (or **models**) to be useful in explaining their behavior? (*Hint:* Fable has it that Sir Isaac Newton was stimulated to develop his theories about the laws of motion as a result of being hit on the head by an apple that had fallen out of the tree under which he was sitting. Did the apple have to understand Newton's theory to behave according to it?)

Part Two

Supply and Demand

INTRODUCTION

The tools of demand and supply are the most basic and useful elements of the economist's kit. Indeed, many economists would argue that the **law of demand**—the lower the price of a good, the greater the quantity of that good demanded by purchasers—is the single most powerful proposition in all of economics. Simply stated, the law of demand has the capacity, unmatched by any other proposition in economics, to explain an incredibly diverse range of human behaviors. For example, the law of demand explains why buildings are taller in downtown areas than in outlying suburbs, and also why people are willing to sit in the upper deck of football stadiums even though lower deck seats are clearly superior. The great explanatory power of the law of demand is almost matched by that of the **law of supply,** which states that the higher the price of a good, the greater will be the quantity of that good supplied by producers. The law of supply helps us understand why people receive a premium wage when they work overtime, as well as why parking places at the beach are so much more expensive during the summer months than they are during the winter.

When the laws of demand and supply are combined, they illuminate the enormous **gains from trade** that arise from voluntary exchange. In Chapter 5, "Sex, Booze, and Drugs," we examine what happens when the government attempts to prohibit the exchanges that give rise to these gains. The consequences are often surprising, always costly, and—sadly—sometimes tragic. We find, for example, that when the federal government made alcoholic beverages illegal during the era known as Prohibition, Americans responded by switching from beer to hard liquor and by getting drunk a larger proportion of the times when they drank. We also show that the government's ongoing efforts to prevent individuals from using drugs such as marijuana and cocaine cause the drive-by shootings that occur in many major cities, and also encourage drug overdoses among users. Finally, we explain why laws against prostitution help to foster the spread of acquired immune deficiency syndrome (AIDS).

In Chapter 6, "Is Water Different?", we dispel the myth that the consumption of some goods does not conform to the law of demand. Here, we examine the demand for water, that "most necessary of all necessities," and find that—lo and behold—when the price of water is raised, people consume less of it—exactly as predicted by the law of demand. One important conclusion of this chapter is that the water shortages and water crises that afflict various parts of the nation are not the result of droughts, but in fact are caused by government officials who are unwilling or unable to accept the reality of the law of demand.

It is surely distasteful to think in terms of the supply and demand for human beings; yet that is what developments half a world away compel us to do in Chapter 7, "Slave Redemption in Sudan." Nearly a century after human slavery was abolished there by British troops, the slave trade has reemerged in Sudan, the largest nation in Africa. Following in the tracks of the slave raiders are slave redemptionists, who seek to alleviate the human suffering in Sudan by purchasing freedom for thousands of enslaved individuals. Yet the efforts of these well-intentioned individuals are having consequences surely not intended by them. Indeed, attempts to reduce slavery in Sudan actually have encouraged the slave trade and even may have resulted in more—not fewer—people in bondage. And so we see that sometimes the consequences of well-intentioned actions are not merely unexpected but tragic as well.

Medical matters form the focus of our analysis in Chapter 8, "Choice and Life," where we look at an issue seemingly unrelated to economics—abortion. Although the debate between a woman's right to choose and a fetus's right to live is usually cast in highly charged, emotional terms, we demonstrate that the dispassionate reasoning of the economist can illuminate some of the issues at stake. Economics can never be the ultimate arbiter of whether abortion should be legal or illegal, but it can help us understand more about what our choices cost.

The cost of a pack of cigarettes in the United States has more than doubled over the last few years, importantly because the federal and state governments have sharply increased cigarette taxes. These tax increases have reduced the supply of cigarettes and so pushed up prices. As we see in Chapter 9, "Smoking and Smuggling," this has led to a host of other developments. The number of smokers and the amount of smoking are both down, as would readily be predicted by the law of demand. Nevertheless, for people who continue to smoke in the face of higher taxes, things are worse: Not only is a larger share of their income going to the "evil weed"; they are also smoking stronger, more carcinogenic cigarettes. At the market level, higher cigarette taxes have also led to much more widespread smuggling of cigarettes, as consumers seek to minimize the costs of the higher taxes. On a variety of fronts, then, we see that the basic tools of supply and demand enable us to understand the sometimes unintended and often surprising economics of public issues.

Wage rates, like all market prices, are determined by the demand and supply of the good in question. In the case of labor, one of the key forces that influence supply is immigration, both legal and illegal. After several decades of decline, immigration into the United States has been rising in recent years. Indeed, it is now at its highest level in more than seventy years. Why this has happened and what effects it will have are the focus of Chapter 10, "Tired, Poor, Huddled Masses." For the economy as a whole, immigration almost certainly yields positive net benefits. Yet immigration potentially also has important effects on the distribution of wealth among individuals. For this reason, and because the benefits produced by immigration are affected by the identity of the immigrants, economic analysis can shed important light on the costs and benefits of alternative immigration policies.

5

Sex, Booze, and Drugs

Prior to 1914, cocaine was legal in this country; today it is not. Alcohol (of the intoxicating variety) is legal in United States today; from 1920 to 1933 it was not. Prostitution is legal in Nevada today; in the other forty-nine states it is not.[1] All these goods—sex, booze, and drugs—have at least one thing in common: The consumption of each brings together a willing seller with a willing buyer; there is an act of mutually beneficial exchange (at least in the opinion of the parties involved). Partly because of this property, attempts to proscribe the consumption of these goods have (1) met with less than spectacular success, and (2) yielded some peculiar patterns of production, distribution, and usage. Let's see why.

When the government seeks to prevent voluntary exchange, it generally must decide whether to go after the seller or the buyer. In most cases—and certainly when sex, booze, or drugs have been involved—the government targets sellers, because this is where the authorities get the most benefit from their enforcement dollars. A cocaine dealer, even a small retail pusher, often supplies dozens or even hundreds of users each day, as did speakeasies (illegal saloons) during Prohibition; a hooker typically services anywhere from three to ten tricks per day. By incarcerating the supplier, the police can prevent several—or even several hundred—transactions from taking place, which is usually much more cost-effective than going after

---

[1] These statements are not quite correct. Even today, cocaine may be legally obtained by prescription from a physician. Prostitution in Nevada is legal only in those counties that have, by virtue of local option, chosen to proclaim it as such. Finally, some counties in the United States remain dry, prohibiting the sale of beer, wine, and distilled spirits.

the buyers one by one. It is not that the police ignore the consumers of illegal goods; indeed, sting operations—in which the police pose as illicit sellers—often make the headlines. Nevertheless, most enforcement efforts focus on the supply side, and so shall we.

Law enforcement activities directed against the suppliers of illegal goods increase the suppliers' operating costs. The risks of fines, jail sentences, and possibly even violence become part of the costs of doing business and must be taken into account by existing and potential suppliers. Some entrepreneurs will leave the business, turning their talents to other activities; others will resort to clandestine (and costly) means to hide their operations from the police; still others will restrict the circle of buyers with whom they are willing to deal to minimize the chances that a customer is a cop. Across the board, the costs of operation are higher, and at any given price, less of the product will be available. There is a reduction in supply, and the result is a higher price for the good.

This increase in price is, in a sense, exactly what the enforcement officials are after, for the consumers of sex, booze, and drugs behave according to the law of demand: The higher the price of a good, the lower the amount consumed. So the immediate impact of the enforcement efforts against sellers is to reduce the consumption of the illegal good by buyers. There are, however, some other effects.

First, because the good in question is illegal, people who have a **comparative advantage** in conducting illegal activities will be attracted to the business of supplying (and perhaps demanding) the good. Some may have an existing criminal record and are relatively unconcerned about adding to it. Others may have developed skills in evading detection and prosecution while engaged in other criminal activities. Some may simply look at the illegal activity as another means of thumbing their noses at society. The general point is that when an activity is made illegal, people who are good at being criminals are attracted to that activity.

Illegal contracts usually are not enforceable through legal channels (and even if they were, few suppliers of illegal goods would be stupid enough to complain to the police about not being paid for their products). Thus, buyers and sellers of illegal goods frequently must resort to private methods of contract enforcement—which often means violence.[2] Hence, people who are relatively good at violence are attracted to illegal activities and are given greater incentives to employ their talents. This is one reason why the murder rate in America rose to record levels during Prohibition (1920–1933) and then dropped sharply when liquor was again made legal. It also helps explain why the number of drug-related murders soared during the 1980s, and why drive-by shootings became commonplace in many drug-infested cities. The Thompson submachine gun of the 1930s and the MAC-10 machine gun of the 1980s were, importantly, just low-cost means of contract enforcement.

The attempts of law enforcement officials to drive sellers of illegal goods out of business have another effect. Based on recent wholesale prices, $50,000 worth of pure heroin weighs about four ounces; $50,000 worth of marijuana weighs about twenty pounds. As any drug smuggler can tell you, hiding four ounces of contraband is a lot easier than hiding twenty pounds. Thus, to avoid detection and prosecution, suppliers of the illegal good have an incentive to deal in the more valuable versions of their product, which for drugs and booze mean the more potent versions. Bootleggers during Prohibition concentrated on hard liquor rather than beer and wine; even today, moonshine typically has roughly twice the alcohol content of legal hard liquor such as bourbon, scotch, or vodka. After narcotics became illegal in this country in 1914, importers switched from the milder opium to its more valuable, more potent, and more addictive derivative, heroin.

The move to the more potent versions of illegal commodities is enhanced by enforcement activities directed against users. Not only do users, like suppliers, find it easier (cheaper) to hide the more potent versions, there is also a change in relative prices due to user penalties. Typically, the law has lower penalties for using an illegal substance than for distributing it. Within each category (use or sale), however, there is commonly the same penalty regardless of value per unit. For example, during Prohibition, a bottle of wine and a bottle of more expensive, more potent hard liquor were equally illegal. Today, the possession of one gram of 90 percent

---

[2] Fundamentally, violence—such as involuntary incarceration—also plays a key role in the government's enforcement of legal contracts. We often do not think of it as violence, of course, because it is usually cushioned by constitutional safeguards, procedural rules, and so on.

pure cocaine brings the same penalty as the possession of one gram of 10 percent pure cocaine. Given the physical quantities, there is a fixed cost (the legal penalty) associated with being caught, regardless of value per unit (and thus potency) of the substance. Hence, the structure of legal penalties raises the relative price of less potent versions, encouraging users to substitute more potent versions—heroin instead of opium, hashish instead of marijuana, hard liquor instead of beer.

Penalties against users also encourage a change in the nature of usage. Prior to 1914, cocaine was legal in this country and was used openly as a mild stimulant, much as people today use caffeine. (Cocaine was even included in the original formulation of Coca-Cola.) This type of usage—small, regular doses over long time intervals—becomes relatively more expensive when the substance is made illegal. Extensive usage (small doses spread over time) is more likely to be detected by the authorities than is intensive usage (a large dose consumed at once), simply because possession time is longer and the drug must be accessed more frequently. Thus, when a substance is made illegal, there is an incentive for consumers to switch toward usage that is more intensive. Rather than ingesting cocaine orally in the form of a highly diluted liquid solution, as was commonly done before 1914, people switched to snorting or even injecting it. During Prohibition, people dispensed with cocktails before dinner each night; instead, on the less frequent occasions when they drank, they more often drank to get drunk. The same phenomenon is observed today. People under the age of twenty-one consume alcoholic beverages less frequently than do people over the age of twenty-one. But when they do drink, they are more likely to drink to get drunk.

Not surprisingly, the suppliers of illegal commodities are reluctant to advertise their wares openly; the police are as capable of reading billboards and watching TV as are potential customers. Suppliers are also reluctant to establish easily recognized identities and regular places and hours of business, because to do so raises the chance of being caught by the police. Information about the price and quality of products being sold goes underground, often with unfortunate effects for consumers.

With legal goods, consumers have several means of obtaining information. They can learn from friends, advertisements, and personal experience. When goods are legal, they can be trademarked for identification. The trademark may not legally be copied, and the courts protect it. Given such easily identified brands, consumers can be made aware of the quality and price of each. If their experience does not meet expectations, they can assure themselves of no further contact with the unsatisfactory product by never buying that brand again.

When a general class of products becomes illegal, there are fewer ways to obtain information. Brand names are no longer protected by law, so falsification of well-known brands ensues. When products do not meet expectations, it is more difficult (costly) for consumers to punish suppliers. Frequently, the result is degradation of and uncertainty about product quality. The consequences for consumers of the illegal goods are often unpleasant, sometimes fatal.

Consider prostitution. In those counties in Nevada where prostitution is legal, the prostitutes are required to register with the local authorities, and they generally conduct their business within the confines of well-established bordellos. These establishments advertise openly and rely heavily on repeat business. Health officials test the prostitutes weekly for venereal disease and every month for AIDS. Contrast this with other areas of the country, where prostitution is illegal. Suppliers generally are streetwalkers, because a fixed, physical location is too easy for the police to detect and raid. Suppliers change locations frequently, to reduce harassment by police. Repeat business is reported to be minimal; frequently, customers have never seen the prostitute before and never will again.

The difference in outcomes is striking. In Nevada, the spread of venereal disease by legal prostitutes is estimated to be almost nonexistent; to date, none of the 9000 registered prostitutes in Nevada has tested positive for AIDS. By contrast, in some major cities outside Nevada the incidence of venereal disease among prostitutes is estimated to be near 100 percent. In Miami, one study found that 19 percent of all incarcerated prostitutes tested positive for AIDS; in Newark, New Jersey, 52 percent of the prostitutes tested were infected with the AIDS virus, and about half of the prostitutes in Washington, D.C., and New York City are also believed to be carrying the AIDS virus. Because of the lack of reliable information in markets for illegal goods, customers frequently do not know exactly what they are getting; as a result, they sometimes get more than they bargained for.

Consider alcohol and drugs. Today, alcoholic beverages are heavily advertised to establish their brand names and are carried by reputable dealers. Customers can readily punish suppliers for any deviation from the expected potency or quality by withdrawing their business, telling their friends, or even bringing a lawsuit. Similar circumstances prevailed before 1914 in this country for the hundreds of products containing opium or cocaine.

During Prohibition, consumers of alcohol often did not know exactly what they were buying or where to find the supplier the next day if they were dissatisfied. Fly-by-night operators sometimes adulterated liquor with methyl alcohol. In extremely small concentrations, this made watered-down booze taste like it had more kick; in only slightly higher concentrations, the methyl alcohol blinded or even killed the unsuspecting consumer. Even in "reputable" speakeasies (those likely to be in business at the same location the next day), bottles bearing the labels of high-priced foreign whiskeys were refilled repeatedly with locally (and illegally) produced rotgut until their labels wore off.

In the 1970s, more than one purchaser of what was reputed to be high-potency Panama Red or Acapulco Gold marijuana ended up with low-potency pot heavily loaded with stems, seeds, and maybe even oregano. Buyers of cocaine must worry about not only how much the product has been cut along the distribution chain, but also what has been used to cut it. In recent years the purity of cocaine at the retail level has ranged between 10 percent and 95 percent; for heroin, the degree of purity has ranged from 5 percent to 50 percent. Cutting agents can turn out to be any of various sugars, local anesthetics, or amphetamines; on occasion, rat poison has been used.

We noted earlier that the legal penalties for the users of illegal goods encourage them to use more potent forms and to use them more intensively. These facts and the uncertain quality and potency of the illegal products yield a deadly combination. During Prohibition, the death rate from acute alcohol poisoning (i.e., due to an overdose) was more than thirty times higher than today. During 1927 alone, 12,000 people died from acute alcohol poisoning, and many thousands more were blinded or killed by contaminated booze. Today, about 3000 people per year die as a direct result of consuming either cocaine or heroin. Of that total, it is estimated, roughly 80 percent die from (1) an overdose caused by unexpectedly potent product, or (2) an adverse reaction to the material used to cut the drug. Clearly, caveat emptor (let the buyer beware) is a warning to be taken seriously if one is consuming an illegal product.

We noted at the beginning of the chapter that one of the effects of making a good illegal is to raise its price. One might well ask, by how much? During the early 1990s, the federal government was spending about $2 billion a year in its efforts to stop the importation of cocaine from Colombia. One recent study concluded that these efforts had hiked the price of cocaine by 4 percent (yes, 4 percent) relative to what it would have been had the federal government done nothing to interdict cocaine imports. The study estimated that the cost of raising the price of cocaine an additional 2 percent would be $1 billion per year.[3]

The government's efforts to halt imports of marijuana have been more successful, presumably because that product is easier to detect than cocaine. Nevertheless, suppliers have responded by cultivating marijuana domestically instead of importing it. The net effect has been an estimated tenfold increase in potency due to the superior farming techniques available in this country, as well as the use of genetic bioengineering to improve strains.

We might also consider the government's efforts to eliminate the consumption of alcohol during the 1920s and 1930s. They failed so badly that the Eighteenth Amendment, which put Prohibition in place, was the first (and thus far the only) constitutional amendment ever to be repealed. As for prostitution—it is reputed to be "the oldest profession," and by all accounts continues to flourish today, even in Newark and Miami.

The government's inability to halt the consumption of sex, booze, or drugs does not in and of itself mean that those efforts have failed. Indeed, the "successes" of these efforts are manifested in their consequences—ranging from tainted drugs and alcohol to disease-ridden prostitutes. The message instead is that when the government attempts to prevent mutually beneficial exchange, even its best efforts are unlikely to meet with spectacular success.

---

[3] Federal attempts to prevent cocaine from entering the country are, of course, supplemented by other federal, as well as state and local, efforts to eradicate the drug once it has crossed our borders. To date, there are no empirical estimates of the extent to which these other efforts have increased prices.

DISCUSSION QUESTIONS

1. The federal government currently taxes alcohol on the basis of the 100-proof gallon. (One-hundred-proof alcohol is exactly 50 percent pure ethyl alcohol; most hard liquor sold is 80 proof, or 40 percent ethyl alcohol, whereas wine is usually about 24 proof and most beer is 6 to 10 proof.) How would alcohol consumption patterns be different if the government taxed alcohol strictly on the basis of volume rather than taking into account its potency as well?

2. During Prohibition, some speakeasy operators paid bribes to ensure that the police did not raid them. Would you expect the quality of the liquor served in such speakeasies to be higher or lower than in speakeasies that did not pay such bribes? Would you expect any systematic differences (e.g., with regard to income levels) among the customers patronizing the two types of speakeasies?

3. When comparing the markets for prostitution in Nevada and New Jersey, there are two important differences: (1) Prostitutes in New Jersey face higher costs because of government efforts to prosecute them; and (2) customers in New Jersey face higher risks of contracting diseases from prostitutes, because the illegal nature of the business makes reliable information about product quality much more costly to obtain. Given these facts, would you expect the price of prostitution services to be higher or lower in New Jersey, compared to Nevada? Which state would have the higher amount of services consumed (adjusted for population differences)?

4. According to the Surgeon General of the United States, nicotine is the most addictive drug known to humanity, and cigarette smoking kills perhaps 300,000 to 400,000 people per year in the United States. Why isn't tobacco illegal in the United States?

6

Is Water Different?

Mono Lake has gotten a reprieve. Over a fifty-year period, this California lake—our country's oldest lake and one of its most beautiful—shrank from more than 80 square miles in area to about 60. Why? Because in 1941, most of the eastern Sierra mountain water that once fed Mono Lake began disappearing down a 275-mile-long aqueduct, south to Los Angeles, where it was used to wash cars, sprinkle lawns, and otherwise lubricate the lifestyle of southern California. Environmentalists cried out that the diversion of water from Mono Lake must stop. Los Angelenos, who pay $350 per acre-foot for the water, claimed there were no viable alternative sources. Central California farmers, who pay but $12.50 per acre-foot for subsidized water from the western side of the Sierras, feared that diverting their own "liquid gold" to save Mono Lake would dry up their livelihood. Meanwhile, this migratory rest stop for hundreds of thousands of birds was disappearing.

Finally, prodded by the California Water Resources Control Board and aided by special funds voted by the state legislature, the City of Los Angeles agreed to drastically curtail its usage of Mono Lake water. Under the water-trading plan agreed to, Los Angeles will cut its usage of Mono Lake water by more than 80 percent until the lake's water level has risen sixteen feet. Even after that elevation has been reached, the city will limit its usage of Mono Lake water to less than half of its long-term average usage. To replace the water it is losing, Los Angeles will buy water from elsewhere, using state funds appropriated for this purpose.

The issues that have arisen over the future of Mono Lake are surfacing in hundreds of locations throughout the United States.

Conservationists are increasingly concerned about the toxic contamination of our water supply and the depletion of our underground water sources. Extensive irrigation projects in the western states use more than 150 *billion* gallons of water a day—seven times as much water as all the nation's city water systems combined. The Ogallala aquifer (a 20-million-acre lake beneath the beef-and-breadbasket states of Colorado, Kansas, Nebraska, New Mexico, Oklahoma, and Texas) has been dropping by three feet per year because 150,000 wells are pumping water out faster than nature can replenish it.

Water problems are not confined to the United States. In China, water is being siphoned away from farmlands surrounding Beijing in order to meet rising urban and industrial demands, and some 400 Chinese cities are now estimated to face water **shortages.** In the arid Middle East, water is a constant source of friction, and schemes to add to the region's supplies have included floating plastic bags of water southward across the Mediterranean, and stirring the sea in the summer in the hopes of causing more rain to fall in the winter. In the island city-state of Singapore, half of the total land area of 247 square miles is set aside for collecting and storing water. Because there is no more room for additional reservoirs, Singapore is now building desalination plants to convert seawater into drinking water. The result will be more water, but the cost of fresh water produced in such a manner is seven to eight times higher than the current cost of treated water.

The common view of water is that it is an overused, precious resource and that we are running out of it. The economic analysis of the water "problem," however, is not quite so pessimistic, nor so tied to the physical quantities of water that exist on our earth and in the atmosphere. Rather, an economic analysis of water is similar to an analysis of any other scarce resource, revealing that water is fundamentally no different from other scarce resources.

The water industry is one of the oldest and largest in the United States, and the philosophy surrounding it merits examination. Many commentators believe that water is unique and that it should not be treated as an **economic good,** that is, a scarce good. Engineering studies that concern themselves with demand for residential water typically use a so-called requirements approach. The forecaster simply predicts population changes and then multiplies those estimates by currently available data showing the average amount of water used per person. The underlying assumption of such a forecast is that, regardless of the price charged for water in the future, the same quantity will be demanded per person. Implicitly, then, both the short- and long-run price elasticities of demand are assumed to be zero.

But is this really the case? Perhaps not. Consider, for example, the cities of Tucson and Phoenix in Arizona. Although these cities are located only 100 miles apart, their water-usage rates are notably different. While the average household in Phoenix uses 260 gallons per day, in Tucson the average usage is only 160 gallons per day. Could this usage difference be accounted for by the fact that the price of water is only about half as much per gallon in Phoenix as it is in Tucson? To see why such an inference is likely correct, let's look at a study of water prices in Boulder, Colorado, conducted by economist Steve Hanke.

Boulder was selected by Hanke because a number of years ago the water utility in Boulder installed water meters in every home and business that it supplied. Prior to that time, Boulder, like many other municipalities in the United States, had charged a flat monthly rate for water. Each household paid a specified amount per month no matter how much (or how little) water was used. In essence, the previous flat-fee system meant that a zero price was being charged at the margin (for any incremental use of water). The introduction of usage meters meant that a positive price for the marginal unit of water was now imposed.

Hanke looked at the quantity of water demanded both before and after the meters were installed in Boulder. He began by computing an index of water usage, relative to what he called the "ideal" use of water. (The term *ideal* implies nothing from an economic point of view. It merely indicates the minimum quantity of water required to maintain the aesthetic quality of each resident's lawn, taking into account such factors as average temperature, the effect of rainfall, and so forth.) An index value of 100 meant that usage was exactly equal to the hypothetical ideal. A value of, say, 150 meant that residents were using 50 percent more than the ideal, whereas an index of 75 meant that usage was 25 percent less than Hanke's ideal figure of 100.

From the data in Table 6–1, which compares water usage in Boulder with and without metering, we find that individuals used much more water under the flat-rate system than they did under the metered-rate system. Column 1 shows the meter route numbers of the eight routes studied by Hanke. Column 2 shows the index of

TABLE 6–1   Comparing Water Usage With and Without Metering of Actual Usage

(1) Meter Routes	(2) Index of Water Usage (Flat-Rate Period)	(3) Index of Water Usage (Metered-Rate Period)
1	128	78
2	175	72
3	156	72
4	177	63
5	175	97
6	175	102
7	176	105
8	157	86

Source: Adapted from Steve Hanke, "Demand for Water Under Dynamic Conditions," *Water Resources Research*, vol. 6, no. 5, October 1970.

water usage for each of the routes during the unmetered period when a flat rate was charged for water usage. The data in column 3 show water usage on each route for the one-year period after the metering system was put into effect. Note that under the flat-rate system every route used substantially more than the ideal amount of water, whereas under the metered system six of the eight routes used less than the hypothetical ideal. Moreover, water usage dropped substantially on every route when metering was introduced, and each user was being charged for the actual amount of water used. Because less water is used in the presence of metering (which raises the price of incremental water), Hanke's data indicate that the quantity of water demanded is a function of the price charged for water. Hanke also found that for many years after the imposition of the metered-rate pricing system for water, the quantity of water demanded not only remained at a lower level than before metering but continued to fall slightly. That, of course, means that the long-run **price elasticity of demand** for water was greater than the short-run price elasticity of demand.

Would attaching a dollar sign to water help solve problems of recurring water shortages and endemic waste? Many economists feel it would. It is well known, for example, that much of the water supplied by federal irrigation projects is wasted by farmers and other users because they have no incentive to conserve water and curb overconsumption. The federal government, which has subsidized water projects since 1902, allots water to certain districts, communities, or farmers on the basis of previous usage "requirements." This means that if farmers in a certain irrigation district were to conserve on water usage by, say, upgrading their irrigation systems, their water allotment eventually would be reduced. As a result, a "use it or lose it" attitude has prevailed among users of federal water. Water supplied by federal water projects is also inexpensive. The Congressional Budget Office has estimated that users pay only about 19 percent of the total cost of the water they get.

One would think that with growing worldwide concern over water conservation, the federal government would be trying to do its part to reduce waste. If anything, the reverse seems to be true. As recently as 1993, Congress authorized completion of the Central Utah Project (CUP), which includes a series of dams, aqueducts, tunnels, and canals designed to collect water from the Colorado River drainage in Utah and transport it to the Great Basin. The cost of delivering this water to farmers for irrigation is estimated to be $400 per acre-foot. The water will be used to produce additional crops yielding enough revenue to make the water worth $30 per acre-foot to the Utah farmers who receive it. But these farmers will pay only $8 per acre-foot for the water—that is, only *2 percent* of the cost of delivering the water to them!

Economists have suggested that raising the price of federal water would lead to more efficient and less wasteful water consumption. For example, a study by B. Delworth Gardner, an economist now at Brigham Young University, concluded that a 10 percent rise in prices could reduce water use on some California farm crops by as much as 20 percent. Support for such a price increase is politically difficult, however, because federal law stipulates that ability to pay, as well as cost, must be considered when determining water prices.

An alternative solution involving the trading and sale of water rights held by existing federal water users has been proposed by some economists. Such a solution, it is felt, would benefit the economy overall because it could help curb water waste, prevent water shortages, and lessen the pressure for costly new water projects. Trading and sales of water rights have already taken place in California, Oregon, and Utah. In addition, environmentalists were instrumental in helping to arrange the water trading plan for Mono

Lake. Despite these modest successes, numerous federal and state laws have, to date, made such trading very difficult. Until recent years, it had been thought that there was so much water we simply did not have to worry about it—there was always another river or another well to draw on if we ran short. Putting a price tag on water would require a substantial change in the way we have traditionally thought about water. Is this possible or even desirable? Well, events half a world away from Mono Lake may shed some light on this. In the Chinese capital of Beijing, an extended period of dry weather in 1997 caused the water levels in the city's reservoirs to drop sharply. The municipal State Council responded by raising the price of water for home use to $110 per acre-foot from its previous level of $80. For industrial and government users, the price hike was to $160 per acre-foot from the previous $125. Why were these actions taken? According to Liu Hangui, deputy director of the Beijing Water Conservancy Bureau, "the price adjustments were introduced to relieve the water shortage." Even communism, it would seem, is not enough to make water different.

DISCUSSION QUESTIONS

1. In your opinion, do the data presented in Table 6–1 refute the "water is different" philosophy?

2. How much water does your neighbor "need"? Is your answer the same if you have to pay your neighbor's water bill?

3. Evaluate the following: "Although taxpayers foot the bill for federal water sold to farmers at subsidized prices, they also eat the crops grown with that water. Because the crops are cheaper due to the subsidized water, taxpayers get back exactly what they put in, and so there is no waste from having subsidized water for farmers." Would you give the author of this quote an A or an F in economics?

4. During the drought that plagued California in the late 1980s and early 1990s, farmers in California were able to purchase subsidized water to irrigate their crops, even though many California homeowners had to pay large fines if they watered their lawns. Can you suggest an explanation for this difference in the treatment of two different groups of citizens within the state of California?

7

Slave Redemption in Sudan

Sudan is Africa's largest nation. Located immediately south of Egypt, it encompasses nearly one million square miles and is home to 35 million people. It is also home to poverty, disease, civil war—and the emergence of modern-day slavery. The slave trade, in turn, has given rise to a new humanitarian movement, whose adherents seek to alleviate Sudan's misery by buying freedom for its slaves. Well-intentioned though they are, these humanitarian efforts may be making things worse.

Slavery is a centuries-old practice in Sudan, one that colonial British rulers finally managed to halt during World War I. The Sudanese gained independence in 1956 but, despite ensuing periods of civil war, the slave trade initially remained a piece of history. This changed in 1989, when the National Islamic Front (NIF) took control of the government. The NIF quickly began arming the Muslim Baggara tribe in the northern part of the country to fight against the rebellious Christian tribes of the south. The Baggara previously had made a regular practice of enslaving members of the southern Dinka tribe, and once armed by the NIF the Baggara resumed the slave raids the British had suppressed. This activity was further aided by the government, which supplied horses to the Baggara and permitted slave markets to open in the cities controlled by the NIF. Perhaps as many as 20,000 Dinkas, mostly women and children, were enslaved and taken north, selling for as little as $15 each. The slaves were branded with the names of their owners and put to work as cooks, maids, field hands, and concubines.[1]

---

[1] See Richard Miniter, "The False Promise of Slave Redemption," *The Atlantic Monthly*, July 1999, pp. 63–70.

Within a few years, word of the revived slave trade began filtering out of Sudan. In response, a variety of humanitarian groups from other nations began buying slaves in large batches and setting them free. The process is called "slave redemption," and its purpose—one hopes—is to reduce the number of people who are enslaved.

Raising money for slave redemption has become big business, spreading rapidly among public schools and evangelical churches. A middle school in Oregon, for example, raised $2500 to be used for slave redemption. Even more impressive was an elementary school class in Colorado: After the children's efforts caught the media's eye, the class raised more than $50,000 for slave redemption.

The largest of the humanitarian groups involved in slave redemption is Christian Solidarity International (CSI). This group says it has freed almost 8000 slaves since 1995, most at prices of about $50 each. In 1999 alone, for example, CSI purchased the freedom of nearly 3000 slaves. Several other groups also purchased the freedom of several hundred slaves that year, sometimes at prices of up to $100 each.

Per capita income in Sudan is about $500 per year, which makes slave prices of $50 to $100 apiece quite attractive to the Baggara slave raiders. This is particularly true when the redeemers are buying in the south, where the targeted Dinkas live, and prices in the north, the traditional market for slaves, are as low as $15 apiece. In fact, says one individual who used to be active in slave redemption, "We've made slave redemption more profitable than narcotics." What are the consequences of such profitability?

There have been two sets of responses. First, on the demand side, the higher prices for slaves make it more costly for owners in the north to hold slaves. So rather than own slaves, some of them have offered their slaves to the redeemers. This, of course, is exactly the effect the slave redemption movement has desired. But there is also a supply response: When the market value of slaves rises due to an increase in demand (the demand of the slave redeemers), we expect an increase in the quantity supplied. That is, we expect the raiders who produce slaves by capturing them to engage in more of that activity. This is exactly what has happened in Sudan.

Slave redemption began in earnest in 1995 and, according to local authorities, the number of slave raids has grown each year since. Moreover, the size of a typical raiding party has grown from roughly

400 attackers to more than 2500. Why the growth? Slaves used to be traded in relatively small batches, but the redeemers prefer to buy in large lots—1000 or more at a time. Collecting and assembling the number of slaves required to satisfy the redemption buyers thus requires considerably more manpower. Hence, the slave trade is gradually being transformed from a cottage industry into a large-scale business enterprise. Overall, it is estimated that the number of slaves captured in raids each year has risen steadily since the inception of slave redemption.

Initially, it is likely that the impact of slave redemption was chiefly on the demand side; that is, the first slaves redeemed were almost surely "freed from slavery" in the sense that we would normally use that terminology. But once the stock of slave holdings in the north had adjusted downward in response to the newly elevated equilibrium price, there was only one place for the slave traders to get the slaves demanded by the redemption buyers. This was from the raiders who were now taking slaves for one purpose only—sale to the redeemers. Thus, once the stock of slaves in the north is adjusted to its lower equilibrium level, *all* of the slaves subsequently "freed" by the redeemers are in fact individuals who never would have been enslaved had the redeemers not first made a market for them. In addition, because large numbers of new slaves now spend some time in captivity awaiting redemption, it is even possible that the total number of people in slavery at any point in time is actually *higher* because of the well-intentioned efforts of the slave redeemers.

As unpleasant as such reasoning is, it agrees with the opinions of people who observe the slave trade firsthand. As a local humanitarian worker says, "[G]iving money to the slave traders only encourages the trade. It is wrong and must stop. Where does the money go? It goes to the raiders to buy more guns, raid more villages. . . . It is a vicious circle." In a similar vein, the chief of one village that has been targeted by the slave raiders says, "Redemption is not the solution. It means you are encouraging the raiders."

In addition to encouraging the capture of new slaves, redemption also reduces any incentive for owners to set free their less productive slaves. Prior to 1995, about 10 percent of all slaves, chiefly older women and young children, were allowed to escape or even told to go home, because the costs of feeding, clothing, and housing them exceeded their value to their owners. Now slaves who would have been freed on their own are instead held in captivity until a trader can be found to haul them south for sale to the redeemers.

The final effect of redemption has been to create a trade in fictitious slaves—individuals who are paid to pose as slaves for the purposes of redemption, and who are then given a cut of the redemption price after they are "freed." Although redemption groups obviously try to avoid participating in such deals, observers familiar with the trade consider them a regular part of the redemption business.

Is there another way to combat slavery in Sudan? On the demand side, the U.S. government has long refused to negotiate with terrorists or pay ransom to kidnappers, simply because it believes that such tactics encourage terrorism and kidnapping. It recognizes that paying a ransom increases the profits of kidnapping, thus enticing more individuals into the trade.

On the supply side, the British were originally successful in ending the slave trade in Sudan and elsewhere in their empire by dispatching soldiers to kill or disarm slave raiders, and by sending warships to close off maritime slave-trading routes. Sudan, of course, is an independent sovereign nation today; both the United Nations and the British electorate would likely oppose unilateral military action by the British government against Sudanese slave raiders. Yet even the people who used to be subject to British colonial rule have mixed feelings. When asked to compare the colonial British policies to the redeemers' policies of today, a schoolmaster in the affected area remarked, "If the colonial government were standing for election, I would vote for them." So too might the victims of the slave trade in Sudan.

DISCUSSION QUESTIONS

1. Is there anything in the historical British experience with the slave trade that suggests how the international community of today could reduce slavery in Sudan?

2. It appears that the actions of the slave redeemers have raised the equilibrium price of slaves. What does this mean has happened to the number of slaves held by private owners in

northern Sudan—as long as the demand for slaves is downward sloping? What does the higher profitability and volume of slave trading today imply about the number of slaves held in inventory in the south for trading purposes, compared to the number that used to be held there?

3. How does the cost of "backhauling" a slave from the north down to the south, where the redeemers are purchasing, affect the extent to which the efforts of the redeemers cause slaves to be released from the existing stock in the north, compared to causing new slaves to be produced in the south?

4. Suppose the redeemers had succeeded in buying slaves without causing the equilibrium price of slaves to change at all. What would this imply about the elasticity of supply of new slaves? What would it imply about the number of slaves actually released from slavery in the north?

8

Choice and Life

The Supreme Court is back in the abortion business. For sixteen years, the Court refused to tamper substantively with its 1973 *Roe* v. *Wade* decision legalizing abortion. But in 1989, in *Webster* v. *Reproductive Health Services,* the Court upheld the constitutionality of a Missouri law restricting, but not eliminating, a woman's right to have an abortion. Then, in a 1992 case, *Planned Parenthood* v. *Casey,* the Supreme Court upheld most of a Pennsylvania law that discourages, but does not prohibit, abortion. Since the *Webster* decision, citizens on both sides of the abortion issue have engaged in legislative battles and sometimes violent public protests over the issue of a woman's right to choose versus a fetus's right to live. Thus far most of the legislative battles have been won by the proponents of legal abortions, but the legal battles and protests continue. It thus seems certain that the Supreme Court will be deciding abortion cases long after you have finished reading this book.

Very few of the major issues of our time are purely economic, and abortion is no exception. Economics cannot answer the question of whether life begins at conception, at twenty-four weeks, or at birth, nor can economics determine whether abortion should be permitted or proscribed. Economics cannot (as yet) even predict how the Supreme Court may ultimately rule on such issues. What economics can do, however, is demonstrate the striking and sometimes surprising implications of the Court's decisions on abortion— whatever those decisions may be.

Pregnancy termination has been practiced since ancient times, and any legal bars to abortion seem to have been based on the father's right to his offspring. English common law allowed abortion before quickening (when fetal movement is first evident), and there is some doubt whether abortion even after quickening was considered a crime. The American colonies retained the tradition of English common law until the changeover to state statutes at the adoption of the Constitution. In 1828, New York enacted an antiabortion statute that became a model for most other states. The statute declared that abortion before quickening was a misdemeanor and abortion after quickening, second-degree manslaughter. In the late nineteenth century, the quickening distinction disappeared and the penalties for all abortions were increased.

Except under extreme circumstances (such as to protect the life of the mother), abortion remained illegal in this country until about 1960, when a few states began to ease the conditions under which it was legal to perform an abortion. The gradual process of liberalization that state legislatures seemed to be following was suddenly disrupted in 1973 with the landmark Supreme Court decision in *Roe* v. *Wade*, which overruled all state laws prohibiting abortion before the last three months of pregnancy. In effect, the Court ruled that a woman's right to an abortion was constitutionally protected except during the last stages of pregnancy. There matters stood until the Supreme Court's 1989 decision in *Webster* v. *Reproductive Health Services.*

Strictly speaking, the Court's decision in *Webster* was narrowly focused; its direct impact has been to permit states to restrict the circumstances under which abortion is legal. Although the *Webster* decision stops far short of overturning *Roe* v. *Wade,* both the subsequent *Planned Parenthood* decision and numerous legislative actions at the state level have further restricted abortion. Examination of the market for abortions during the period prior to *Roe* v. *Wade* will help clarify the economic consequences of these developments.

Consider first the factors of cost and risk. During the early 1970s, an illegal but otherwise routine abortion by a reputable physician in the United States typically cost a minimum of $3500 (in 2001 dollars) and could run $5000 in a major East Coast City.[1] Following *Roe* v. *Wade*, these prices dropped sharply, and by the time of *Webster*, a routine legal abortion performed during the first

---

[1] All of the dollar amounts mentioned in this chapter are adjusted for **inflation** and expressed in terms of 2001 dollars, for purposes of comparison.

three months of pregnancy cost only about \$350.[2] Prior to the legalization of abortion, more than 350,000 women were admitted annually to American hospitals with complications resulting from abortions, and it is estimated that more than 1000 women per year died from improperly performed pregnancy terminations. Following the Court's 1973 decision, complications and deaths from pregnancy termination dropped sharply. In recent years, it is estimated that significant physical complications occur in less than 1 percent of all legal abortions, and deaths due to legal abortions are virtually unknown. In short, the legalization of abortion was associated with a drastic reduction in both the monetary costs and physical dangers of pregnancy termination. Why was such an association observed?

Let us begin by looking at who might be willing to perform an illegal abortion and the price at which she or he would be willing to perform it. A physician convicted of performing an illegal abortion faced not only criminal prosecution (and the associated costs of a legal defense) but also expulsion from the medical profession and the consequent lifetime loss of license and livelihood. In addition, the doctor may have had to endure ostracism by a community that regarded abortion as a criminal act. In short, the costs to a doctor of such a criminal conviction were enormous, and the greatest portion of the fee for an illegal abortion was simply compensation for bearing this potential cost.

It must be acknowledged, of course, that there were physicians who had strong moral convictions regarding a woman's right to abortion. Some were willing to absorb the risks of performing an illegal abortion at a substantially reduced fee. Nevertheless, such physicians were a small minority and not easy to find. Consequently, most women were faced with the choices of paying \$3500 or more for an abortion, paying \$700 to \$900 to an unlicensed abortionist operating under unsanitary conditions, or simply doing without. For those choosing back-alley abortionists, the consequences could include infection, hospitalization, sterility, or death.

The illegality of abortions, of course, increased the cost both of supplying and obtaining information about them; in turn, this made decisions about whether to have an abortion and who should per-

---

[2] More complicated abortions, performed as late as the fifth or sixth month of pregnancy, cost \$1200 to \$1400 if done on an outpatient basis in a clinic, and \$1600 to \$2000 if performed in a hospital.

form it more difficult and increased the chances of an undesirable outcome. Information is never free, even in legalized activities, because it costs money to acquaint potential buyers with the location, quality, and price of a good or service. But, as mentioned in Chapter 5, in the case of an illegal activity the provision of information is even more expensive. Abortionists could not advertise, and the more widely they let their availability be known, the more likely they were to be arrested. Although some doctors unwilling to perform abortions did refer patients to other, more willing physicians, the referral was itself illegal and therefore risky. Women seeking an abortionist thus were not able to inform themselves of all of the possibilities without spending large amounts of money and time; and even having done so, many were left facing enormous uncertainty about the best path. Some ended up spending too much money; others exposed themselves to unnecessary risks. Some might even have chosen not to have an abortion had they been fully informed of the potential risks.

The situation confronting women during the years prior to the legalization of abortion can be usefully categorized by considering three examples. Although the settings are stylized, they are representative of the nature of the choices involved and the costs and risks of each.

First, there is a wealthy entertainer who visits a travel agency that arranges a package tour of Japan. Included is round-trip airfare, an essentially risk-free abortion procedure in that country (where abortions are legal), and several days of subsequent sightseeing. The price tag: $7500.

Next, let's look at how a young attorney earning $48,000 per year resolves her dilemma. She goes to her physician, who on the quiet refers her to a doctor willing to perform an illegal abortion in his office for $3500. The expense forces the attorney and her husband to delay the purchase of their first home, but then so would the cost of having the baby.

Finally, there is a blue-collar couple making $24,000 a year. Surreptitiously asking around, the wife finds out from an acquaintance that the local barber will do the abortion in a back room for $900—aspirins, but not antibiotics, included.

For the wealthy entertainer, both the risk and the financial burden are negligible; to be sure, the money could have been spent on an expensive bauble, but at least there was a trip to Japan in return.

For the young lawyer, the financial burden is considerable; if unpaid law school debts preclude either the physician-performed abortion or the cost of completing the pregnancy, the only alternative is the risk of the backroom abortionist. The blue-collar couple gets the worst of both worlds: The abortionist's fee pushes them over their already tight budget, and the woman risks hospitalization or worse.

The pattern suggested by these examples was borne out in the years preceding the legalization of abortion. Relatively few women had the resources permitting travel to a foreign country where abortion was both safe and legal, nor did many have access to the information needed to learn about and arrange such an undertaking. Somewhat more women had established relationships with physicians who either would perform abortions or could refer them to other, willing doctors; these women had the option of choosing between the higher expense of the physician or the greater risk of the unlicensed abortionist. For many women, however, the lack of readily available information about alternatives, combined with the high costs of a physician-performed abortion, meant that the backroom quack, with the attendant risks, was the only realistic means of terminating a pregnancy.

The statistics for New York City in the early 1960s support this argument: Private hospitals performed abortions on 1 pregnant patient in 250; municipal hospitals, 1 in 10,000. The rate for whites was five times that for nonwhites and thirty times that for Puerto Ricans. Lower-income women simply were not having as many abortions performed by qualified physicians in suitable surroundings as were upper-income women; as we noted earlier, the result was hundreds of thousands of abortion-related complications, plus more than 1000 deaths each year.

The legalization of abortion in 1973 brought a relatively swift end to such outcomes. No longer faced with the risk of losing liberty and livelihood, thousands of physicians became willing to perform abortions. Even those who, for moral or religious reasons, were unwilling to terminate pregnancies could refer patients to other physicians without legal risk to themselves. Within a short time, properly equipped abortion clinics were established, and even in states requiring that abortions be performed in hospitals, women found a greatly increased range of options. Legalization thus produced an enormous increase in the supply of pregnancy termination services, which in turn had several consequences.

As in any market in which there is an increase in supply, the price of abortions fell drastically; holding quality and safety constant, the price reduction was as much as 90 percent. The decline in the price of physician-supplied abortions to levels at or below those charged by back-alley abortionists quickly drove most of the quacks out of business. As a result, the safety of abortions increased dramatically; serious infections and deaths due to abortion are estimated to have declined by 50 percent within a year of *Roe* v. *Wade* and have since become quite rare. Information about abortions, once available only "on the sly" and at considerable trouble and expense, became openly available. A woman considering pregnancy termination could call her physician's office or simply look in the telephone book for information about local services. Moreover, not only was knowledge about the price, quality, and safety of abortion openly available, so too were counseling services about the potentially adverse psychological or emotional consequences of what, for many women, was a difficult and trying decision.

As would be expected, the lower price of abortion and the more widely available information about the procedure combined to bring about a large increase in the number of abortions performed in this country. During 1973, slightly over 700,000 legal abortions were performed in the United States, many of them in the aftermath of the Supreme Court's landmark decision. One early study concluded that of the legal abortions that took place in the year following *Roe* v. *Wade,* "well over half—most likely between two-thirds and three-fourths . . . were replacements for illegal abortions."[3] By 1981, 1.6 million legal abortions per year were being performed in the United States. After holding steady at that rate until 1988, the number of abortions performed each year began a slow decline, reaching about one million in 2000.

What then have been the consequences of the Court's decision in *Webster*? In the short run, not much. To be sure, abortions in public facilities in Missouri are now illegal, and women in the later stages of pregnancy must undergo costly and risky tests regarding fetal viability before having an abortion. Thus the Court's decision

---

[3] June Sklar and Beth Berkov, "Abortion, Illegitimacy, and the American Birth Rate," *Science*, vol. 185, September 13, 1974, pp. 914ff.

has increased the costs of pregnancy termination in Missouri. The result has been fewer abortions, perhaps some illegal abortions, and the selection of more effective means of (prepregnancy) birth control. Nevertheless, there are good (albeit more expensive) substitutes available—abortions in private facilities or in neighboring states—so that the magnitude of these effects has been small. Of more significance is that the Court's decision, combined with growing public opposition to abortion, has encouraged numerous states to restrict abortions. For example, at least seventeen states now have three or more abortion restrictions, up from three states in 1992. Indeed, in 1997 alone, states passed a record fifty-five abortion restrictions, ranging from parental consent laws to outright bans on certain forms of late-term abortions. Conditions thus are gradually moving toward those that prevailed before 1973: Abortions are becoming more expensive and more are probably being performed illegally and less safely. As was the case before 1973, the burden of these consequences will be borne largely by women in the middle- and lower-income brackets.

We emphasized at the beginning of this chapter that the issues raised by abortion go far beyond the economic consequences, and that economics cannot, in any event, determine whether abortion should be permitted or proscribed. What economics can do—as we hope we have shown—is to illustrate some of the consequences of the decision between "choice" and "life." Whether an understanding of those consequences can—or even should—play a role in making that decision is a matter we can leave only to the reader.

DISCUSSION QUESTIONS

1. Suppose you wished to predict which states would impose more restrictive conditions on abortions. What factors—for example, per capita income and average age of the population—would you take into account in making your predictions?

2. Before 1973, legal penalties generally were imposed on suppliers of abortion rather than on demanders. How might the effects of prohibiting abortion been different had legal penalties been imposed on demanders rather than on suppliers?

3. The discussion in this chapter focused solely on the economic consequences of prohibiting abortion. Do you think that legislatures base their decisions about abortion solely on the economic consequences? Can an understanding of the economic consequences of laws give us (and legislatures) any guidance about the "best" public policy on abortion?

4. As of 2000, it was up to the states to decide on public policy regarding abortion. Some people have argued that the federal government (perhaps through a Constitutional amendment) should decide on a uniform national policy regarding abortions. What are the advantages and disadvantages of having separate state policies rather than a uniform national policy?

9

Smoking and Smuggling

Cigarette taxes have been in the news lately, and for good reason: Federal taxes per pack jumped a dime to 34 cents in 2000, and are scheduled to go up again in 2002. Meanwhile, a majority of the states either have instituted their own tax increases or have such hikes on the legislative agenda. Indeed, over the last five years, higher federal and state taxes have helped double the average price of a pack of cigarettes in the United States.

A variety of motives is pushing the increase in tax rates. Partly, the higher taxes are an effort to reduce smoking, particularly among young people. Taxpayers often end up paying the tobacco-induced medical bills of smokers, through Medicare (for the elderly) and Medicaid (for the poor). Reducing the number of smokers, it is argued, will help cut these costs. In addition, given the current low state of public opinion about smoking, cigarette taxes are proving to be a politically palatable way of raising tax revenues. Sometimes (as in California) these receipts are used in part to fund antismoking advertising campaigns; other times (as has been proposed in New York) cigarette tax receipts are seen as a source of funds for publicly provided health care initiatives.

There is little doubt that, despite the addictive attributes of nicotine, higher cigarette taxes make inroads on smoking—after all, the demand curve for cigarettes, like the demand curve for any other good, is downward sloping. For each 10 percent that taxes push up the retail price, the number of packs sold drops by 4 to 8 percent. Interestingly, however, although smokers respond to higher taxes by smoking fewer cigarettes, they also tend to smoke cigarettes that are longer and have higher nicotine and tar content. This effect is so pronounced among people aged 18 to 24 that the average daily tar intake among the young people who continue to smoke is actually higher when the tax rate is higher. Because tar is believed to be the principal carcinogenic substance in cigarettes, higher taxes probably lead to *more* adverse health consequences among young smokers.

Smoking tends to be concentrated among lower-income individuals, which means that the burden of cigarette taxes also tends to be concentrated in this segment of the population. For example, one survey several years ago revealed that only 19 percent of people earning more than $50,000 per year smoked, whereas 32 percent of those earning less than $10,000 smoked. As a result, cigarette taxes consumed 0.4 percent of the income of smokers in the high-income group but an amazing 5.1 percent of the income of the low-income smokers. Indeed, it is estimated that more than half the latest increase in federal taxes will be borne by people earning less than $25,000 per year.

Perhaps the most interesting consequence of changes in cigarette taxes, however, is the change in distribution channels that results. Cigarettes are both light and compact relative to their market value, and this becomes increasingly important when the taxes on them are raised. Thus, cigarettes are prime candidates for smuggling—and taxes are a prime stimulus to such smuggling. Worldwide, of the 1 trillion cigarettes exported in 1999 from producing nations, it is estimated that 280 billion were sold by smugglers, up from 100 billion in 1989. The chief reason for this smuggling is that cigarette taxes vary enormously around the world, creating price differences across nations of several dollars per pack.

For example, in Britain, where cigarettes cost about $5.50 per pack, it is estimated that one-half of all British smokers consume at least some smuggled cigarettes each year. About one in four cigarettes consumed in Spain are illegal, 20 percent of Italian cigarettes are black market, and perhaps 40 percent of all cigarettes consumed in Hong Kong are contraband. In low-tax Luxembourg, it is estimated that only 15 percent of tobacco purchased is consumed in-country—with the rest being moved covertly to higher-tax locales elsewhere in Europe.

In 1991 the Canadian federal government raised cigarette taxes by 146 percent, yielding a price per pack of $3.50, compared to an average U.S. price of $1.00 at the time. Provincial governments soon followed suit with higher cigarette taxes of their own. By 1994, black market cigarette consumption in Canada had jumped to 25 percent of total consumption, up from about 2 percent. How did this happen? When Canadian cigarettes are exported, they are exempt from Canadian cigarette taxes. Soon after the higher federal and provincial taxes went into effect, there was a huge rise in (tax-exempt) exports to the United States, where the cigarettes were promptly—and illegally—reexported back to Canada. The federal and provincial goverments ultimately were forced to slash their taxes down to about what they had been before the smuggling outbreak.

How big are the potential cigarette smuggling stakes in the United States? With an average $1.00-per-pack hike in combined state and federal taxes—a number that is not unlikely by the end of 2001—the potential net revenue to smugglers would be on the order of $3 billion to $6 billion per year, even if only a quarter of all smokers turned to the black market. And where would these smuggled cigarettes come from? Almost anywhere. Mexico, a transshipment point for much of America's illegal drug imports, is one possibility. Between 1989 and 1995, U.S. exports of cigarettes to Mexico went from 5 million packs a year to 150 million. Some of this surely was due to increased Mexican consumption, but a significant amount is believed to be due to reexports to California: In 1989 that state had raised cigarette taxes to 35 cents a pack from 10 cents a pack. Other likely sources of smuggled cigarettes are domestic U.S. military bases and Indian reservations, where cigarettes are tax-exempt. Both of these venues have been sources of bootleg cigarettes in the past, when combined federal and state taxes were far lower than they are now.

The potential problems facing states when they raise their cigarette taxes are magnified by the fact that other states represent potential sources of supply. Economists Daniel K. Benjamin and William R. Dougan of Clemson University have studied the role of bootleg cigarettes in shaping cigarette taxes around the country. They have found that cigarette smuggling is highly sensitive to interstate tax differentials of only a few cents per pack, and that state governments are thus forced to consider the taxing behavior of other states or suffer the consequences.[1] For example, the late 1940s

---

[1] Daniel K. Benjamin and William R. Dougan, "Efficient Excise Taxation: The Evidence from Cigarettes," *Journal of Law & Economics*, April 1997 pp. 113–136.

saw an outbreak of smuggling when a significant number of states first began using cigarettes as a source of tax revenue. Another outbreak of smuggling occurred in the 1970s as states raised taxes to make up for other revenue losses caused by the recession of the early 1970s.

Recent experience in Michigan suggests that the latest round of state cigarette tax increases can be expected to produce yet another epidemic of interstate smuggling. In 1994 Michigan hiked its tax to 75 cents per pack from 25 cents. At the time, this gave it the second-highest state cigarette tax in the nation. Within just over a year, 20 percent of the cigarettes consumed in Michigan were smuggled in, as smokers traveled to Ohio and Indiana to save more than $6.00 (about one-third) on the cost of a carton. There has been sharp rise in organized, large-scale heists of cigarettes from convenience stores, and even a major law enforcement push against cigarette bootlegging seems unable to quell the onslaught of illegal imports.

None of these developments would be surprising to the British, who two centuries ago relied on import tariffs to fund much of their government spending and suffered the consequences. Between 1698 and 1758 the standard tariff rate went from 10 percent to 25 percent. After further increases in tariffs during the American Revolution, smuggled goods accounted for a full 20 percent of all imports to Britain. Tea was particularly popular and thus heavily taxed. Indeed, the tax rate reached 119 percent, and by 1784 it was estimated that two-thirds of all tea consumed in Britain was contraband. Given the direction that cigarette taxes are headed, cigarette smuggling seems headed the same way.

DISCUSSION QUESTIONS

1. Various state and federal laws specify that a pack of cigarettes contains twenty cigarettes, and that these cigarettes are limited in the total amount of tobacco they may contain. If such limits were not in place, when taxes per pack were raised, what would you expect to see happen to the number of cigarettes in a pack and the amount of tobacco in a cigarette?

2. In a world where transportation costs are positive, what effect would distance from the point of production be expected to have on the size of the tax that a state would find appropriate to levy on a pack of cigarettes?

3. In 1978, interstate trucking was deregulated in the United States, leading to greater competition in this industry and lower freight rates. In light of your answer to question 2, what effect would you expect trucking deregulation to have on the interstate pattern of cigarette taxes? In particular, what would happen to taxes in states distant from the major point of production in North Carolina, relative to taxes in states closer to North Carolina?

4. Cigarettes that are smuggled from North Carolina to New York must pass through Virginia, Maryland, Delaware, and New Jersey along the way. Suppose that authorities in Delaware decide to raise taxes in the hope of discouraging smoking. What impact would this Delaware tax hike have on cigarette taxes in New York and New Jersey, compared to cigarette taxes in Maryland and Virginia?

10

Tired, Poor, Huddled Masses

Despite the Statue of Liberty's justly famous welcome to America's newcomers, immigration remains a lightning rod for political and social controversy. Much of the debate focuses on illegal immigration: How should we prevent it, and how should we respond when people illegally succeed in breaching our shores? But much of the debate also has addressed whether *any* immigration into the United States should be permitted, and if so, just who should be granted that right.

The issue of immigration has gained far more attention in recent years because of the upsurge in it since the 1960s. There are 27 million or so foreign-born persons now in America—almost 10 percent of the total population. Nevertheless, measured as a proportion of the population, immigrants are far less significant than they were in years past. Between 1880 and 1920, for example, foreign-born persons typically comprised 15 percent of the population. Subsequent legal restrictions reduced the influx of immigrants sharply, leading to a forty-year decline in the proportion of the U.S. population that was foreign-born. It has only been in the last thirty-five years that the foreign-born proportion has begun to rebound.

This rebound was itself caused by a change in federal immigration policy. In 1965, perhaps influenced by the mood of the civil rights movement, the United States started to eliminate quotas that favored white Europeans. Instead, the federal government made family unification the centerpiece of immigration policy. As a result, children, spouses, and siblings poured in from around the world to join immigrants who originally had entered alone. This flood was further stimulated by growing sentiment that individuals fleeing communist persecution should receive special status as refugees. Additional entry visas were set aside for such refugees, pushing immigration totals above what they would have been. Most immigration—two-thirds or more—is legal, so we shall begin by looking at the effects of immigration in general. By definition, immigration entails an influx of individuals from other locations. The inflow stimulates both the supply of labor and the demand for goods and services. In labor markets, although the overall result will be a rise in total employment, the new arrivals also may tend to depress wage rates. This is said to be a particular concern in markets for low-skilled jobs because of the lower average skills possessed by new immigrants. If immigration depresses wage rates in these markets, some native-born workers may become unemployed or drop out of the labor force altogether. Much of the adverse sentiment toward immigration has been stimulated by this potential negative impact on low-skilled American workers.

Superficially, at least, there appears to be some basis for this concern. Most new immigrants are clearly committed to making their way in the labor force: The Urban Institute estimates, for example, that about 74 percent of adult male immigrants hold jobs, versus 72 percent of the overall male population. A number of studies have examined whether this influx of immigrant workers has adversely affected native-born workers; all of the researchers have come to essentially the same conclusion—little or no negative impact on employment or unemployment rates of less-skilled natives.

There are at least two possible reasons for the minimal adverse impact of immigrants on native workers. First, the demand for unskilled labor may be highly elastic; that is, the quantity demanded may be quite responsive to even small changes in wages. Under such circumstances, an increase in the supply of labor results chiefly in a rise in employment, rather than a wage decrease that would push native-born workers out of employment. Second, new immigrants seem to compete chiefly for low-skilled jobs with other immigrants, not with Americans. The garment industry of New York is a prime example: Recent arrivals from Latin America, the Caribbean, and the Far East sit at machines once operated by Italians and Jews. On balance, then, the arrival of new immigrants boosts employment overall. For example, in examining the 400 largest counties in the

United States, one study found that for every 100-person increase in the population of adult immigrants, the number of new jobs rose by 46, while for every 100 new native-born Americans, the number of new jobs rose by just 25.

On the demand side of the market, many immigrants initially have relatively low incomes and thus are most likely to consume basic staple items, such as food, used cars, and inexpensive clothing. But—and this is a key source of contention in those areas of the country that have received the brunt of immigration—new immigrants are also likely to be consumers of publicly provided or subsidized services, such as public transportation, education, and some forms of health care. Indeed, the adverse impact that new immigration sometimes has on state and local budgets is often its most visible and easily quantifiable measure and therefore an important source of opposition to immigration. At times, this opposition can reach extraordinary lengths. Thus in California, voters passed a ballot initiative that sought to strip illegal immigrants of rights to many expensive government services, including education and nonemergency health care.

With a million or so immigrants streaming into the United States each year, the potential fiscal burden on government, particularly at the state and local level, is considerable. As we shall see, there is merit to the concerns over the cost to taxpayers of new immigration. Yet this concern is also somewhat misplaced.

One measure of the potential adverse impact of immigration lies in the fact that foreign-born households are significantly more likely to receive public assistance. But the behavior of immigrants is far from uniform in this regard. Roughly two-thirds of all immigrants arrive legally under the regular immigration system. They generally are well educated and highly motivated, and are only moderately more likely than natives to receive welfare payments. It seems clear that these individuals contribute positively to the fiscal well-being of government at all levels, paying more in taxes than they receive in government benefits.

The story is much different for the other one-third of all immigrants (comprised of illegal immigrants, as well as legal immigrants arriving as refugees from former communist countries). The refugees in particular impose a significant drain on government coffers. Overall, receipt of welfare among refugees is double that of other legal immigrants; among recent refugee arrivals, roughly one-third are on welfare. Although illegal immigrants typically may not receive any cash assistance, many are regular consumers of other forms of taxpayer-funded public assistance. One study estimated, for example, that during the early 1990s a majority of the births in the Los Angeles area were to illegal immigrant mothers, paid for chiefly with public funds.

The sharp difference in behavior between refugees and illegal immigrants on the one hand, and regular immigrants on the other hand, is probably due in part to the illegal immigrants' and refugees' lower educational levels (and thus lower earning capacity) than those of either regular-status immigrants or native-born individuals. But at least as important regarding the behavior of refugees are the sharp differences in government policy toward regular and refugee immigrants. For example, regular-status immigrants are not eligible for welfare until they have been in the country for at least five years. In contrast, refugees from countries such as Laos, Cambodia, Vietnam, the former Soviet Union, and Cuba are immediately eligible for a wide range of benefits exceeding even what native-born Americans get.

Whatever immigrant groups we are discussing, California is likely to figure prominently in the debate. This is hardly surprising, because more new immigrants live in California than in any other state. On the illegal immigration front, California is even more of a national leader. Of the 5 million or so illegal immigrants who are estimated to reside in the United States, nearly 2 million of them—about 40 percent—are believed to live in the Golden State.

Given the prominence of California in the immigration debate, it is useful to ask why so many immigrants—particularly illegal immigrants—have been attracted there. Partly the answer is geography. California not only shares a border with Mexico, it also has a vast shoreline and major ports that beckon potential arrivals from the Far East. Also important, however, is that the flood of immigrants to the Golden State, particularly illegal immigrants, has been the result of policies pushed for by Californians. For example, in 1984 and 1985, Los Angeles, San Francisco, and many other municipalities in California declared their cities to be sanctuaries for illegal immigrants from Central American governments that were regarded as centers of political repression. Then, in 1986, the California congressional delegation held up passage of the Immigration and Reform Act until a provision was added to allow several hundred thousand immigrants into the country temporarily so that they could help harvest crops, predominantly in agriculture-rich California.

Under the so-called guest worker provisions that eventually resulted, about 1.1 million immigrants entered the United States and won legal status. Most of them settled in California, attracted by wages that were up to ten times as high as those payable in their countries of origin. These new legal immigrants proved a powerful attraction for their families, who soon began arriving in large—and chiefly illegal—numbers. The women and children who comprised these families were the ones most likely to use government services such as education and health care. Thus as the deputy chief of staff to the California governor noted, when it comes to illegal immigration, "in some ways there have been self-inflicted wounds."

DISCUSSION QUESTIONS

1. Why are the opponents of immigration likely to be more vocal than are the supporters of immigration?

2. How do the costs of immigration change relative to the benefits as the value of publicly provided or subsidized services rises in real terms?

3. What would happen to the composition of immigrants if, as suggested by Nobel prize-winning economist Gary Becker, the United States began auctioning off entry visas to potential immigrants who were willing and able to pay the most money for the right to enter the country legally?

4. If one perceived communist countries to be a threat to the United States, would it make good economic sense to offer special refugee status to persons emigrating from communist nations?

Part Three

Nonprice Rationing

INTRODUCTION

Although monetary prices are the most commonly used instrument of rationing in a market economy, they are not the only means. A key productive feature of government is its role in defining and enforcing property rights so that market prices can perform their role in allocating scarce resources. But sometimes—for any of a variety of reasons—government seeks to prevent monetary prices from doing their job. At other times, the government seems unable or unwilling to create or to define the property rights necessary for prices to achieve maximum effectiveness. In either case, we still live in a world of scarcity, so rationing must still take place. A variety of instruments may perform the rationing functioning, and in this section we examine many of them. Along the way we find that nonprice rationing is both more costly and more complex than most people ever imagined.

Our first look at nonprice rationing comes in Chapter 11, "Bankrupt Landlords, from Sea to Shining Sea." Here we examine the effects of **rent control**—a legal ceiling on the rent that landlords may charge for apartments. As with many of the issues we consider in this book, the effects of rent controls are more surprising, and costly, than you might think. We find, for example, that legal ceilings on rents have increased the extent of homelessness in the United States, have led to a rise in racial discrimination, and have caused the wholesale destruction of hundreds of thousands of dwelling units in our nation's major cities. We cannot escape one simple fact: Politicians may pass legislation, and bureaucrats may do their best to enforce it, but the laws of demand and supply ultimately rule the economy.

Perhaps not surprisingly, many of the same people who argue that rent controls should be used to ensure "affordable housing" also advocate that the government should guarantee access to "affordable health care." Despite their laudable goals, it turns out that, once again, achieving them is rather more difficult than it might seem. As we see in Chapter 12, "Rationing Health Care," in response to the high cost of medical care, many nations have tried to remove health care from the marketplace. Yet the fundamental problems of scarcity remain: Producers must be rewarded for their efforts, and consumers' otherwise unlimited desires somehow must be rationed. In the market system, prices perform these functions. But under the systems of government-mandated, universal health care that now exist (or are likely to exist), suppliers are directed by government edict and prices no longer ration demand. Instead, these systems rely on another method of rationing, called "rationing by waiting" because people are forced to wait—weeks or even months—for whatever level of medical care is offered to them. Under such a system, the costs of health care are clearly different than they are under a market system, but it is not clear that they are any lower.

A "living wage" is yet another social goal that seems unassailable yet proves to be surprisingly elusive. In Chapter 13, we examine "The Effects of the Minimum Wage" and find once again that the effects of government actions are not always what they seem, nor are they usually what their proponents claim for them. The chief losers in minimum wage hikes are often the very people who can least afford those losses, while those who claim to support the law on altruistic grounds are in fact likely to be the biggest winners. The message of this chapter may well be this simple piece of advice: When someone claims to be doing something *for* you, it is time to ask what that person is doing *to* you.

Our final foray into nonprice rationing takes place on the road—sitting somewhere in a traffic jam. Travel on most roads in the United States (and elsewhere in the world) is "free," in the sense that one does not have to pay a direct monetary price to commute to work or to take a Sunday drive. Yet as we see in Chapter 14, "Caught in Traffic," roads are in fact scarce goods, meaning that their usage ultimately must be rationed by something. In most places in the world, during parts of most days, the scarce space on roads is rationed by the valuable time of drivers, in the form of traffic congestion. Traffic jams not only yield economic losses that are avoidable, advancing technology is making it increasingly easy to avoid those losses. Yet governments seem reluctant to take advantage of that technology. In examining the reasons for that reluctance, we come to a better understanding of why, despite the great advantages of having prices ration scarce goods, we often choose instead to rely on nonprice rationing.

11

Bankrupt Landlords, from Sea to Shining Sea

Take a tour of Santa Monica, a beachfront enclave of Los Angeles, and you will find a city of bizarre contrasts. Pick a street at random, and you will likely find run-down rental units sitting in disrepair next to homes costing $500,000. Try another street, and you will find abandoned apartment buildings adjacent to luxury car dealerships and trendy shops that sell high-fashion clothing to Hollywood stars. Sound strange? Not in Santa Monica—known locally as the People's Republic of Santa Monica—where stringent rent control laws have routinely forced property owners to leave their buildings empty and decaying rather than even bothering to sell them.

Three thousand miles to the east, rent control laws in New York City—known locally as the Big Apple—are forcing landlords to abandon housing units because the owners no longer can afford the financial losses imposed by rent control. Largely as a result of such abandonments, the city government of New York owns more than 150,000 derelict housing units—empty, except for rats and small-time cocaine dealers. Meanwhile, because the controls also discourage new construction, the city faces a housing gap of 200,000 rental units—apartments that easily could be filled at current controlled rental rates, if the units existed in habitable form.

From coast to coast, stories like these are commonplace in the 200 or so American cities and towns that practice some form of rent control—a system in which the local government tells building owners how much they can charge for rent. Time and again, the stories are the same: poorly maintained rental units, abandoned apartment buildings, tenants trapped by housing gridlock in apartments no longer suitable for them, bureaucracies bloated with rent control enforcers, and even homeless families that can find no one who will rent to them. Time and again, the reason for the stories is the same: legal limits on the rent that people may pay for a place to live.

Our story begins in 1943, when the federal government imposed rent control as a temporary wartime measure. Although the federal program ended after the war, New York City continued the controls on its own. Under New York's controls, a landlord generally could not raise rents on apartments as long as the tenants continued to renew their leases. Rent controls in Santa Monica are more recent. They were spurred by the inflation of the 1970s, which, combined with California's rapid population growth, pushed housing prices and rents to record levels. In 1979, the city of Santa Monica (where 80 percent of the residents are renters) ordered rents rolled back to the levels of the year before and stipulated that future rents could go up by only two-thirds as much as any increase in the overall price level. In both New York and Santa Monica, the objective of rent controls has been to keep rents below the levels that would be observed in freely competitive markets. Achieving this goal has required that both cities impose extensive regulations to prevent landlord and tenant from evading the controls—regulations that are costly to enforce and that distort the normal operation of the market.

It is worth noting that the rent control systems in New York and Santa Monica are slowly yielding to decontrol. For a number of years, some apartments in New York have been subject only to "rent stabilization" regulations, which are somewhat less stringent than absolute rent controls. In addition, New York apartments going for over $2000 per month are deregulated when a lease ends. In Santa Monica, the state of California mandated that, effective in 1999, newly vacant apartments are no longer subject to the city's rent control ordinance. Even so, in both cities, the bulk of the rental market is dominated by rent controls, and so we focus on the consequences of those controls.

In general, the unfettered movement of rental prices in a freely competitive housing market performs three vital functions: Prices allocate existing scarce housing among competing claimants; they promote the efficient maintenance of existing housing and stimulate the production of new housing, where appropriate; and they ration usage of housing by demanders, thereby preventing waste of scarce housing. Rent control prevents rental prices from effectively performing these functions. Let's see how.

Rent control discourages the construction of new rental units. Developers and mortgage lenders are reluctant to get involved in building new rental properties because controls artificially depress the most important long-run determinant of profitability—rents. Thus, in one recent year, 11,000 new housing units were built in Dallas, a city with a 16 percent rental vacancy rate but no rent control statute. In that same year, only 2000 units were built in San Francisco, a city with a 1.6 percent vacancy rate but stringent rent control laws. In New York City, the only rental units being built are either exempt from controls or are heavily subsidized by the government. Private construction of new apartments in Santa Monica also dried up under controls, even though new office space and commercial developments—both exempt from rent control—were built at a record pace.

Rent control leads to the deterioration of the existing supply of rental housing. When rental prices are held below free market levels, property owners cannot recover through higher rents the costs of maintenance, repairs, and capital improvements. Thus such activities are sharply curtailed. Eventually, taxes, utilities, and the expenses of the most rudimentary repairs—such as replacing broken windows—overwhelm the depressed rental receipts; as a result, the buildings are abandoned. In New York, some owners have resorted to arson, hoping to collect the insurance on their empty rent-controlled buildings before the city claims them for back taxes. Under rent controls in Santa Monica, the city insisted that owners wishing to convert empty apartment buildings into other uses had to build new rental units to replace the units they no longer rented. At a cost of up to $50,000 per apartment, it is little wonder that few owners were willing to bear the burden, choosing instead to leave the buildings empty and graffiti-scarred.

Rent control impedes the process of rationing scarce housing. One consequence of this is that tenant mobility is sharply restricted. Even when a family's demand for living space changes—due, for example, to a new baby or a teenager's departure for college—there can be substantial costs in giving up a rent-controlled unit. In New York City, landlords often charge "key money" (a large, up-front cash payment) before a new tenant is allowed to move in. The high cost of moving means that large families often stay in cramped quarters whereas small families, or even single persons, reside in very large units. In New York, this phenomenon of nonmobility has come to be known as *housing gridlock*. In Santa Monica, many homeowners rented out portions of their houses in response to soaring prices in the 1970s and then found themselves trapped by their tenants, whom they could not evict even if they wanted to sell their homes and move to a retirement community.

Not surprisingly, the distortions produced by rent control lead to efforts by both landlords and tenants to evade the rules. This in turn leads to the growth of cumbersome and expensive government bureaucracies whose job is to enforce the controls. In New York, where rents can be raised when tenancy changes hands, landlords have an incentive to make life unpleasant for tenants or to evict them on the slightest pretense. The city has responded by making evictions extremely costly for landlords. Even if a tenant blatantly and repeatedly violates the terms of a lease, the tenant cannot be evicted if the violations are corrected within a "reasonable" time period. If the violations are not corrected—despite several trips to court by the owners and their attorneys—eviction requires a tedious and expensive judicial proceeding. For their part, tenants routinely try to sublet all or part of their rent-controlled apartments at prices substantially above the rent they pay the owner. Because both the city and the landlords try to prohibit subletting, the parties often end up in the city's Housing Courts, an entire judicial system developed chiefly to deal with disputes over rent-controlled apartments.

Strict controls on monthly rents force landlords to use other means to discriminate among prospective tenants. Simply to ensure that the rent check comes every month, many landlords rent only to well-heeled professionals. As one commentator put it, "There is no disputing that Santa Monica became younger, whiter, and richer under rent control." The same pattern occurred under the rent control laws of both Berkeley, California, and Cambridge, Massachusetts.

There is little doubt the bureaucracies that evolve to administer rent control laws are cumbersome and expensive. Between 1988 and 1993 New York City spent $5.1 billion rehabilitating housing confiscated from private landlords. Even so, derelict buildings continued piling up at a record rate. The overflow and appeals from the city's Housing Courts clog the rest of New York's judicial system, impeding the prosecution of violent criminals and drug dealers. In Santa Monica, the Rent Control Board began with an annual budget of $745,000 and a staff of twenty people. By the early 1990s, the staff had tripled in size and the budget was pushing $5 million. And who picked up the tab? The landlords did, of course, with an annual special assessment of $200 per unit levied on them.

Ironically, the big losers from rent control—in addition to landlords—are often low-income individuals, especially single mothers. Indeed, many observers now believe that one significant cause of homelessness in cities such as New York and Los Angeles is rent control. Often, poor individuals cannot assure the discriminating landlord that their rent will be paid on time—much less paid—each month. Because controlled rents generally are well below free-market levels, there is little incentive for apartment owners to take a chance on low-income individuals as tenants. This is especially true if the prospective tenant's chief source of income is a welfare check. Indeed, a significant number of the tenants appearing in New York's Housing Courts have been low-income mothers who, due to emergency expenses or delayed welfare checks, have missed rent payments. Often their appeals end in evictions and new homes in temporary public shelters or on the streets. Under Santa Monica rent controls, some owners who used to rent one- and two-room units to welfare recipients and other low-income individuals simply abandoned their buildings, leaving them vacant rather than trying to collect artificially depressed rents that failed to cover operating costs. The disgusted owner of one empty and decaying eighteen-unit building had a friend spray-paint his feelings on the wall: "I want to tear this mess down, but Big Brother won't let me." Perhaps because the owner had escaped from a concentration camp in search of freedom in the United States, the friend added a personalized touch: a drawing of a large hammer and sickle, symbol of the former Soviet Union.

It is worth noting that the ravages of rent controls are not confined to capitalist nations. In a heavily publicized news conference several years ago, the foreign minister of Vietnam, Nguyen Co Thach, declared that a "romantic conception of socialism" had destroyed his country's economy after the Vietnam War. Mr. Thach stated that rent control had artificially encouraged demand and discouraged supply, and that all of the housing in Hanoi had fallen into disrepair as a result. Thach concluded by noting, "The Americans couldn't destroy Hanoi, but we have destroyed our city by very low rents. We realized it was stupid and that we must change policy."

Apparently, this same thinking was what induced the state of California to call a halt to Santa Monica's rent control ordinance, mandating that newly vacant apartments be free of controls. The result of that policy change was an almost immediate jump in rents, as well as a noticeable rise in the vacancy rate—both exactly what we would expect to occur with decontrol. Interestingly enough, however, prospective new tenants were less enthusiastic about the higher rents than many landlords had expected. The reason? Well, twenty years of rent controls had produced that many years of reduced upkeep, and thus apartments that were, well, less than pristine. As one renter noted, "The trouble is, most of this area . . . [is] basically falling apart." And another complained, "I don't want to move into a place that's depressing, with old brown carpet that smells like chicken soup." Higher market rents will eventually change both the ambiance and the aroma of Santa Monica apartments—but only at the same rate that the market is allowed to perform its functions.

DISCUSSION QUESTIONS

1. Why do you think governments frequently attempt to control apartment rents but not house prices?

2. What determines the size of the key money payments that landlords demand (and tenants offer) for the right to rent a controlled apartment?

3. Who, other than the owners of rental units, loses as a result of rent controls? Who gains from rent controls? What effect would the imposition of rent controls have on the market price of an existing single-family house? What effect would rent controls have on the value of vacant land?

4. Why do the owners of rental units reduce their maintenance expenditures on the units when rent controls are imposed? Does their decision have anything to do with whether they can afford those expenditures?

12

Rationing Health Care

Americans spend a larger share of national income on health care—more than 14 percent—than any other people of the world. Moreover, for almost every one of the last twenty years, the price index for medical care has increased more rapidly than the price index for all goods and services in general. With spending on health care at record high levels, it is little wonder that some political leaders have labeled health care in the United States a "crisis." The national debate reached a fever pitch back in 1994 because President Bill Clinton had made government-mandated universal health care coverage one of the pillars of his legislative program. Although no legislation passed during Clinton's presidency the debate over universal health care coverage resumed in earnest during the 2000 elections. It is instructive to look at what has happened in other countries that have adopted some form of a national health care system.

We obviously cannot cover every aspect of health care here, nor can we demonstrate that one system of health care delivery is better than another one. What we can do, however, is to note the consequences of this critical point: In a world of scarcity, some form of rationing is inevitable. In the market system, that rationing is done by prices. Under the systems of government-mandated universal health care that now exist (or are likely to exist in the future), prices are not permitted to ration demands. Instead, these systems rely on another system of rationing: It is called *rationing by waiting,* because people are forced to wait—for weeks or months—for whatever level of medical care is offered them.

The most common form of government-mandated universal health care coverage found in the world today is the single-payer health care system that in essence offers universal health care to consumers at a money price of zero. (The term *single-payer* is used because the government writes the checks for the medical bills.) Britain offers a typical example. The British National Health Service (NHS) has been in existence since 1948. Once touted as one of the world's best national health care examples, the NHS has deteriorated dramatically. Consider hospital beds: In 1948 there were ten hospital beds per thousand people. Today there are about five per thousand people. Since 1948 about 50 percent of Britain's hospitals have been closed for "efficiency" reasons—meaning that the British government cannot or will not afford to keep them open. Britain now has fewer hospital beds per capita than every Western European country except Portugal and Spain.

Because patients in Britain do not pay directly for the services they receive, some other means of rationing must be used. In Britain, the rationing device is waiting, and as the number of hospital beds and other medical facilities have been cut relative to the population, it is little surprise that waiting times have increased. Currently more than a million British patients are waiting for hospital admission. Many others do not show up on waiting lists because they simply do not apply, knowing that the wait is so long. In some London hospitals, individuals routinely spend more than 12 hours waiting to see a physician.

The total staff in the NHS has, in contrast, skyrocketed. Whereas in 1948 the staff-to-bed ratio was .73 to 1 for each hospital bed, today it is 3.1 to 1 for each hospital bed; even with the drop in beds per capita, there are now twice as many staff members for each patient as there were in 1948. One would expect this would enhance medical care. Unfortunately, however, the staff, for the most part, do not deal directly with the treatment of patients. Rather, they have become part of the NHS bureaucracy. This is because the government-run NHS adds a new department or committee for every new aspect of medicine that develops. The NHS consists of a bureaucratic network unknown in the decentralized medical system in the United States.

The national health care system in Canada offers another example. In essence, under the Canadian system the government picks up the entire tab for all covered medical procedures. Currently, only 11 percent of Canada's national health care spending goes to administration, compared to 24 percent in the United States. Canada devotes 9.5 percent of its national income to health care, about a third less than in the United States. Perhaps because of the seemingly low cost of the Canadian system, many supporters of health care reform in the United States often point to Canada's system as one that the United States should emulate.

One impact of the lower level of spending in Canada is that their system does not provide the latest in medical technology. Although Canada ranks fifth highest among developed nations in health care spending as a share of income, it ranks in the bottom third of those countries in availability of technology. For example, compared to the United States, on a per capita basis Canada has far fewer CAT scan and magnetic resonance imaging (MRI) machines, critical in performing sophisticated, difficult diagnostics. Similarly, Canadian medical facilities have almost none of the medical devices needed to remove kidney stones without painful and dangerous surgery. Moreover, operating rooms in Canada operate on strict financial budgets and are allowed to continue operating only if they are within those monthly budgets. What happens if an operating room exhausts its budget on, say, the 20th of the month? It shuts down until the beginning of the next monthly budget cycle.

The costs to the users of the Canadian system show up in other ways as well. Two Canadian economists, Cynthia Ramsay and Michael Walker of the Fraser Institute in British Columbia, have studied the waiting times across a variety of medical specialties. They discovered that many Canadians each year were not permitted to enter the hospital when they or their physician deemed best; instead they had to wait until facilities became available. Moreover, Canadians typically were not even able to get in to see their doctors when they wanted. Ramsay and Walker measured the delay from the time that a primary care physician referred a patient until a specialist actually treated the patient; they found that the demand for health care was rationed by waiting. Listed in Table 12–1 are the average waiting times in weeks for the services of various medical specialists. The three columns show the waiting times for Canada as a whole and the waiting times in individual Canadian provinces that had, respectively, the shortest and longest waiting times.

TABLE 12–1   Average Waiting Time for Treatment by a Specialist
in Canada

(In Weeks)

Specialty	Shortest Wait	Longest Wait	Canada Average
Orthopedics	10.3	39.7	25
Plastic Surgery	9.1	40.5	19.8
Ophthalmology	8.1	39	22.3
Gynecology	5.5	27.2	13.1
Otolaryngology	8.3	26	14.4
Urology	8.2	29.2	12.6
Neurosurgery	10	31	17
General Surgery	6.2	22.3	9.2
Internal Medicine	4.6	7.2	6.4
Cardiovascular	12.5	31.5	17.9

Source: The Fraser Institute, Vancouver, BC, Canada.

Two facts are apparent from Table 12–1. First, it is commonplace for Canadians to have to wait three or four months to receive
health care that is anything beyond that offered by a nurse or primary care physician. Second, the Canadian system produces huge
inequalities in the way people are treated, not only across illnesses,
but also across provinces for the same illness. These long waits, and
the extent of unequal treatment, have produced a regular stream of
Canadians who come to the United States and spend their own
money for medical care here, rather than await their fate at home.
The waiting in Canada has gotten so bad that some provincial governments ship heart bypass patients and cancer patients needing radiation over the U.S. border to receive treatment. Although this is
politically unpopular with the Canadian federal government, the alternative, it seems, is to let the patients die at home, waiting.

Another example of government-controlled health care involves the Netherlands. The government there decides on global
budgets to control hospital expenditures. It also limits the number

of doctors who may specialize in a given area and caps the number of patients they may see. In addition, the government controls physician fees. To help the government meet its budgets, many medical specialists have simply stopped working as much as they used to work. It is commonplace for highly trained surgeons to work only half days or to take weeks off at the end of the year. The result is that typically there is about a three-month waiting list for coronary bypass surgery. Over 15 percent of the patients on the waiting list die before the operation can be performed. Diabetics wait an average of three months to obtain laser treatment for retinal hemorrhaging—and risk blindness in the process. The average wait for removal of gallbladder stones and repairs of hernias is from four to eight weeks. Some forms of reconstructive surgery require waits of up to four years.

Under Dutch law, companies must pay employees' salaries for the first two to six weeks of an illness, depending on the size of the company. This has generated an interesting incentive: The companies have discovered that they can reduce their costs by renting hospital rooms that they keep open for their employees. The companies thus do not have to pay employee salaries while they wait—disabled—for treatment. Although the Dutch system is supposed to provide equal treatment for all, treatment in fact has come to depend on the size and influence of the company for which a person works.

Although our analyses have involved three foreign countries, we need go no further than our own Veterans Administration (VA) to find similar examples. The Veterans Administration operates a 100 percent government-owned and financed health care system. It is the largest health care system in our country and one of the largest in the world. It has 171 medical centers with over 80,000 beds. It operates 362 outpatient and community clinics that receive 23 million patient visits a year. In addition, it has 128 nursing homes with over 70,000 patients. All of the states, plus the District of Columbia and Puerto Rico, have at least one VA medical center, and the VA boasts almost 250,000 employees nationwide.

The General Accounting Office (GAO) did a study of the VA a few years ago, concluding that the VA system faces a growing demand for "free" medical services. Herein lies the rub—the quantity demanded of most services at a zero price will almost always exceed the quantity supplied. Consequently, because price is not used as a rationing device, some other method must be used to ration the scarce resources. Fifty-five percent of the patients who use the VA for routine medical problems wait three hours or longer and sometimes an entire day in order to be seen for a few minutes by a VA general physician. Even among patients requiring urgent medical care, one in nine must wait at least three hours. Patients in need of specialized care cannot even be *seen* by a specialist for 60 to 90 days. They wait months more if surgery or other special procedures are required.

Whether the location is Britain, Canada, Holland, or even the U.S. Veterans Administration, when prices are prevented from clearing the market for medical care, waiting time is the most commonly used means of rationing demand. As one unidentified U.S. veteran told the GAO, "I pack a lunch and take a book." Another veteran, retired 69-year-old Army Major Elmer Erickson, stated, "Be prepared to spend the day there. You will eventually see a doctor."

DISCUSSION QUESTIONS

1. Suppose we had government-mandated universal access to food. How would the outcome likely differ from what is observed with health care systems of this type?

2. Under the Canadian system, those Canadians who are dissatisfied with the health care they receive can come to the United States for medical care if they can afford it. If the United States adopted a system similar to Canada's, where could Americans go if they were not satisfied with the medical care they were receiving?

3. Under the current U.S. health care system, insurance companies often perform the role performed by government agencies under the British, Canadian, and Dutch systems—they pay the bills and they limit the care that people are able to consume. Why might health insurance companies be expected to do a better job in performing these functions than would a government agency?

4. How much health care do people "need"? Does this amount depend on the cost of providing it?

13

The Effects of the Minimum Wage

Ask workers if they would like a raise and the answer is likely to be a resounding yes. But ask them if they would like to be fired or have their hours of work reduced and they would probably tell you no. The effects of the minimum wage are centered on exactly these points.

Proponents of the **minimum wage**—the lowest hourly wage firms legally may pay their workers—argue that low-income workers are underpaid and unable to support themselves or their families. The minimum wage, they say, raises earnings at the bottom end of the wage distribution, with little or no disruption to workers or businesses. Opponents claim that most low-wage workers are low-skilled youths without families to support. The minimum wage, it is said, merely enriches a few teenagers at the far greater expense of many others, who can't get jobs. Most important, opponents argue, is that many individuals at the bottom end of the economic ladder lack the skills needed for employers to hire them at the federal minimum. Willing to work but unable to find jobs, these individuals never learn the basic on-the-job skills needed to move up the economic ladder to higher-paying jobs. The issues are clear—but what are the facts?

The federal minimum wage was instituted in 1938 as a provision of the Fair Labor Standards Act (FLSA). It was originally set at $0.25 per hour, about 40 percent of the average manufacturing wage at the time. Over the next forty years, the legal minimum was raised periodically, roughly in accord with the movement of market wages throughout the economy. Typically, its level has averaged between

40 percent and 50 percent of average manufacturing wages. In response to the high inflation of the late 1970s, the minimum wage was hiked seven times between 1974 and 1981, reaching $3.35 per hour—about 42 percent of manufacturing wages. Ronald Reagan vowed to keep a lid on the minimum wage, and by the time he stepped down as president, the minimum's unchanged level left it at 31 percent of average wages. In 1989, after vetoing a hike in the minimum wage to $4.55 per hour, President Bush signed legislation that raised the minimum to $3.80 in 1990 and $4.25 in 1991. Five years later, at the urging of President Clinton, Congress raised it in two steps to $5.15 per hour. By the time you read this, it is likely that the minimum wage will have been increased again.

About 4 million workers earn the minimum wage; another 2 million or so take home even less because the law doesn't cover them. Supporters of the minimum wage argue that it prevents exploitation of employees and helps them earn enough to support their families and themselves. Even so, at $5.15 per hour, a full-time worker earns only about 60 percent of what the government considers enough to keep a family of four out of poverty. In fact, to get a family of four with one wage earner up to the poverty line, the minimum wage would have to be over $8.00 per hour.

Yet those who oppose the minimum wage argue that such calculations are irrelevant. For example, two-thirds of the workers earning the minimum wage are single, and they earn enough to put them above the poverty cutoff. Moreover, about half of these single workers are teenagers, most of whom have no financial obligations, except possibly for their clothing and car insurance expenditures. Thus opponents argue that the minimum wage chiefly benefits upper-middle class teens who are least in need of assistance at the same time that it costs the jobs of thousands of disadvantaged minority youths.

A few researchers dispute the contention that the minimum wage costs some individuals their jobs. Nevertheless, the overwhelming evidence on this issue points to a negative impact of the minimum wage on employment. After all, the number of workers demanded, like the quantity demanded for all goods, responds to price: the higher the price, the lower the number desired. There is, however, general debate over *how many* jobs are lost due to the minimum wage. For example, when the minimum wage was raised from $3.35 to $4.25, credible estimates of the number of potential job losses ranged from 50,000 all the way up to 400,000. When the minimum was hiked to $5.15, researchers suggested that at least 200,000 jobs were at stake. With a workforce of 135 million persons, numbers like these may not sound very large. But most of the people who don't have jobs as a result of the minimum wage are teenagers; they comprise only about 5 percent of the workforce but bear almost all of the burden of foregone employment alternatives.

Significantly, the youths most likely to lose work as a result of the minimum wage are disadvantaged teenagers, primarily minorities. On average, these teens enter the workforce with the fewest job skills and the greatest need for on-the-job training. Until and unless these disadvantaged teenagers are allowed to acquire these skills, they are the most likely to be unemployed as a result of the minimum wage—and thus least likely to have the opportunity to move up the economic ladder. With a teen unemployment rate better than triple the overall rate, and unemployment among black youngsters hovering above 30 percent, critics argue that the minimum wage is a major impediment to long-term labor market success for minority youth.

Indeed, the minimum wage has an aspect that not many of its supporters are inclined to discuss: It can make employers more likely to discriminate on the basis of sex or race. When wages are determined by market forces, employers who would discriminate on the basis of sex or race face a reduced, and thus more expensive, pool of workers. But when the government mandates an above-market wage, a surplus of low-skilled workers results, and it becomes easier and cheaper to discriminate. As U.S. Treasury Secretary Lawrence Summers noted, the minimum wage "removes the economic penalty to the employer. He can choose the one who's white with blond hair."

Critics of the minimum wage also argue that it makes firms less willing to train workers lacking basic skills. Instead, companies may choose to hire only experienced workers whose abilities justify the higher wage. Firms are also likely to become less generous with fringe benefits in an effort to hold down labor costs. The prospect of more discrimination, less job training for low-skilled workers, and fewer fringe benefits for entry-level workers leaves many observers uncomfortable. As economist Jacob Mincer of Columbia

University notes, the minimum wage means "a loss of opportunity" for the hard-core unemployed.

The last time Congress and the President agreed to raise the minimum wage, it was only after a heated battle lasting months. Given the stakes involved—an improved standard of living for some, a loss of job opportunities for others—it is not surprising that discussions of the minimum wage soon turn to controversy. As one former high-level U.S. Department of Labor official has said: "When it comes to the minimum wage, there are no easy positions to take. Either you are in favor of more jobs, less discrimination, and more on-the-job training, or you support better wages for workers. Whatever stance you choose, you are bound to get clobbered by the opposition." And whenever the Congress and the President face this issue, one or both parties usually feel the same way.

DISCUSSION QUESTIONS

1. Are teenagers better off when a higher minimum wage enables some to get higher wages but causes others to lose their jobs?

2. Are there methods other than a higher minimum wage that could raise the incomes of low-wage workers without reducing employment among minority youngsters?

3. Why do you suppose that organized labor groups, such as unions, are consistent supporters of a higher minimum wage, despite the fact that their members all earn much more than the minimum wage?

4. Is it possible that a higher minimum wage could ever *raise* employment?

14

Caught in Traffic

If you've ever been caught in a rush hour traffic jam, you understand what happens when a scarce good has a price of zero. In this case, the scarce good is highway travel, and when the monetary price of travel is zero, something else must be used to ration the quantity of the good demanded. During rush hour (and much of the rest of the day in places like Los Angeles, New York, Seattle, and Atlanta) the "something" that rations travel demand is time—the time of the motorists caught in traffic.

Whenever a person drives a car, he or she generates a variety of costs. First are the private costs of driving—fuel, oil, vehicular wear and tear, and the value of the driver's time.[1] These costs are all borne by the driver. As a result, when deciding whether and how much highway travel to consume, the driver weighs these costs against the benefits of that travel. If these were the only costs of driving—and on some roads at some times they are—then this chapter would end here. Drivers would bear the full cost of their activities, just as the consumers of pizza do, and there would be no further issues to consider. But the fact is that in most places of the world, during parts of most days, driving generates another cost—congestion—which is not borne by the individuals responsible for it.

On any road, after traffic volume reaches a given level, additional cars entering the road slow the flow of traffic. Once this congestion occurs, every additional car slows traffic even more.

[1] Ideally, the excise tax on fuel, as well as automobile licensing fees, are set to accurately reflect the costs of maintaining and policing the road system. Hence drivers pay not only for their vehicles and their time, they also pay for roads and the police necessary to keep them safe.

Eventually, traffic may even come to a complete halt. Under these circumstances, each driver is implicitly using, without paying for it, a valuable resource that belongs to other people—the time of other drivers. Unless drivers are somehow made to bear the congestion costs they create, we know that two things must be true: First, the monetary price of traveling on the road is too low, and second, the value of motorists' time spent in traffic must be rationing the quantity of travel demanded.

Why do economists worry about congestion? Because its existence raises the possibility that too many people are trying to use the road, and that those people could actually be made *better off* if they were somehow charged a monetary price for using the road. This monetary price would induce fewer motorists to drive—some would carpool, others would use public transit, and still others might telecommute rather than come into the office at all. The reduced driving would reduce congestion and so conserve the valuable time of those people who continued to drive. In fact, it is even possible that by charging drivers a monetary fee or "toll" to drive on a road, *more* people would succeed in reaching their destination in any given time period. It is easiest to see this when traffic is so bad that it comes to a grinding halt. The toll would discourage some people from entering the road and so permit the remaining traffic to move and thus reach its destination. But the general principle is there even when traffic is just badly slowed by the congestion: Road tolls can both improve traffic flow and make drivers better off.

Why, then, do we not see more widespread use of tolls on highways? There are three reasons. First, toll collection is not free, and until recently the costs were often large enough to offset many of the benefits. If you've ever traveled on a toll road such as the Pennsylvania or New Jersey turnpikes, you have some notion of these costs: Not merely must the toll booths be constructed and manned twenty-four hours a day, traffic must come to a halt to pay the toll. This, of course, creates more of the congestion that the tolls are supposed to relieve.

Over the last decade, electronic toll collection systems have been developed that reduce these costs substantially. Small, inexpensive electronic devices called transponders can be installed in cars that will be using the toll road. The transponders transmit identifying information to receivers at the toll stations, which are suspended above the roadway. (The toll stations are also equipped with cameras to record the license plate number of anyone passing through with a missing or malfunctioning transponder.) Cars need not even slow down from cruising speeds to have their identification recorded as they pass through. Then, at the end of the month each motorist receives a bill in the mail for their toll charges (or a ticket if they've tried to avoid the toll). Clearly, this sort of system is designed for roads or bridges heavily trafficked by regular commuters, but in such circumstances, such as on the bridges in the New York City area, electronic toll collection has drastically lowered the costs of using monetary prices to ration roadway usage. The result has been reduced congestion and improved economic efficiency. Drivers are better off and local governments have extra revenue to spend on other services.

The second impediment to pricing highway travel is the often radical and unpredictable consequences of changes in the cost of travel. Unlike a typical privately provided good, each road is part of a network of roads; a change in costs on one segment of the system can sometimes have striking and substantial consequences elsewhere—consequences that can largely or completely offset the benefits of the tolls.

The island nation of Singapore, for example, has some of the worst traffic in the world, and so has been experimenting with pricing roads for many years. As long ago as 1975, Singapore began charging a special fee for vehicles entering the central business district during peak traffic periods. When combined with other traffic control measures, the fee helped cut traffic in central Singapore by 45 percent during peak hours, enabling traffic speed to almost double to about 22 miles per hour. But these positive effects in the central city between 7:30 A.M. and 9:30 A.M. had harmful effects elsewhere. For example, just outside the central city, traffic jams got worse, as drivers sought routes they could use without paying. Moreover, on the roads leading into the central city, the drop in rush hour traffic was nearly matched by a sharp increase in traffic just before 7:30 A.M. and after 9:30 A.M.

There were other costs as well. People who had been long-time bus riders, for example, found that their commuting time went up and comfort down, as former car commuters began jamming the buses to avoid the congestion charge. Subsequent studies of the system also revealed that the fees charged for central city access were actually too high, rather than too low as before. The result was that the valuable city center roads had become underutilized: The inefficiency of too much traffic had been replaced by the inefficiency of too little.

Still, Singapore has continued to modify its system, hoping to learn from its mistakes. The use of transponders has permitted more precise pricing of road space, for example, reducing the adverse consequences of tolls. Moreover, the private sector is providing potential new solutions. The network aspects of roads have many similarities to those of telephone systems and the Internet. Private firms are rapidly learning more about how to price their networks, and that information is sure to improve the pricing of road networks in Singapore and elsewhere.

Perhaps the biggest impediment to efficient pricing of roads, however, is that roads typically are operated by governments rather than by private sector firms. Decisions to price roads must pass through the political process—which necessarily means that the efficiency concerns of the economist are likely to be outweighed by political concerns over who shall pay how much for what. Public opinion polls from densely populated and heavily congested Hong Kong help us understand the consequences.

Although motorists and nonmotorists in Hong Kong are almost identical in agreeing that traffic congestion is serious (84.5 percent and 82.0 percent, respectively), they differ sharply in what they think should be done about it. Motorists favor new road construction, presumably because this would shift part of the cost of relieving congestion to tax-paying nonmotorists. In contrast, nonmotorists believe that financial disincentives to driving (such as tolls and licensing fees) should be given the top priority, presumably because this would shift more of the burden to drivers. Despite Hong Kong's justifiable reputation as a hotbed of capitalism, these divergences of public opinion have slowed the use of private sector remedies for the congestion on publicly owned roads, just as they have elsewhere in the world. The result is too few roads on which monetary prices are too low—and thus congestion is too high.

So where does this put you, caught in a traffic jam somewhere? Advances in electronic road pricing and in our understanding of network management are sure to speed the spread of pricing to highways. But the fundamental fact remains that as long as highway decision making is a product of the political system rather than the market place, rationing by waiting on highways is likely to be with us.

DISCUSSION QUESTIONS

1. Some localities use means other than tolls to reduce congestion on major routes. For example, some use access-limiting traffic lights at freeway on-ramps. From an economist's perspective, what are the disadvantages of such a system?

2. Suppose that when you ate a pizza you had to pay for the crust but not the toppings. What would happen to the number of pizzas you ate and the amount and quality of the toppings you ordered on each?

3. Referring back to question 2, after you had fully adjusted to a price of zero for toppings, what would be the marginal value to you of the last topping consumed? (You can give an exact number.) Does this equal the marginal cost of the last topping, assuming that toppings are a scarce good? Are you consuming the efficient number of toppings? Of pizzas?

4. If the purpose of a toll is to bring the private costs of a driver's actions into equality with the social costs, should the size of the toll depend on how many passengers are in the car? Should it depend on the size of the car (or differ between cars, trucks, and buses)? Should it depend on the time of day that it is collected?

Part Four

MARKET STRUCTURES

INTRODUCTION

The competitive model employed in our discussion of demand and supply assumes that firms on both sides of the market satisfy the conditions of **pure competition**. For sellers of goods, this means the demand curve they face is **perfectly elastic**: Suppliers must take the market price as given, because any attempt by them to raise their price above the market price will result in the loss of all of their sales. Similarly, purchasers in the competitive model face a supply curve that is also perfectly elastic. The market price is given, and any attempt by them to purchase at less than that price will be unsuccessful—no one will sell to them.

The conditions of pure competition imply that buyers and sellers have no effect individually on market prices. Even a casual glance at the world suggests that the conditions of pure competition are not always met. Sometimes, as is the case for major corporations, the firms are large enough relative to the market that significant changes in their purchase or sale decisions clearly must have an effect on prices. In other cases, buyers or sellers are somehow "unique," in that no other buyer or seller offers exactly what they do. (Classic examples include the superstars of sports and entertainment, who will sell less of their services if they raise their prices, but will still sell some.) Sometimes firms that otherwise would be pure competitors join to form a **cartel**, acting as a single decision-making unit whose collective output decisions affect the market price.

When a seller's decisions affect the price of a good, economists usually call the firm a **monopoly**. Literally, this means "single seller," but what is actually meant is that the firm faces a downward-sloping demand curve for its output, so that its decisions affect the price at which its output is sold. When a buyer's decisions affect the market price, we term the firm a **monopsony**, or "single buyer." This just means that the firm faces a positively sloped supply curve, so that its purchasing decisions affect the price at which it buys goods. (Some economists use the term **price searcher** to mean any firm—buyer or seller—whose decisions affect market prices, and who must there-fore search for (or decide on) the price that maximizes the firm's profits. Following this terminology, a pure competitor would be called a **price taker**, for such a firm takes the market price as given.)

The starting point for our examination of different market structures, Chapter 15, "The E-commerce Explosion," provides a look at the incredibly rapid growth of commercial activity on the Internet. Many economists believe that the conditions for the model of pure competition are met here as well as they are in almost any market. On-line auctions, such as those conducted by eBay.com, cer-tainly seem to satisfy the conditions of pure competition, although of course traditional price searchers are also free to sell their goods over the Internet. The possibility of shopping around the world from one's desktop computer promises to enhance competition and reduce search costs, but that process is far from complete. Indeed, price dispersion on the Net seems every bit as widespread as it is on Main Street. And although the growing use of automated search agents ("bots") will likely increase competition and reduce price dispersion, no one really knows yet what long-term impact the Internet will have on market structures.

A major player on the Internet (and just about everywhere else in the personal computer world) is software giant Microsoft—a price searcher if ever there was one. Indeed, concerned that the company was acting in ways that would be harmful to others, the U.S. Justice Department sued the company for violating antitrust laws. As we see in Chapter 16, "Pity the Poor Monopolist," although the government convinced the judge that Microsoft was a monop-oly, the trial left open the issue of whether it was consumers or perhaps just competitors that Microsoft had harmed. In the fast-changing world of computers, by the time the government finally decides what to do with Microsoft, the structure of the market may have changed so much as to make the entire exercise pointless.

It was Microsoft's competitors who apparently convinced the Justice Department to sue Microsoft, presumably because they did not like the company's brand of competition. There is little doubt that if Microsoft is seriously hampered by the government's lawsuit, competitors will be important beneficiaries. As we see in Chapter 17, "Keeping the Competition Out," enlisting the government to hamstring or exclude competitors is probably the most reliable means of ensuring that you are protected from the rigors of competition. Perhaps for this reason, the array of markets in which the government stifles competition is nothing short of remarkable. Here we examine just a handful, ranging from taxicabs to hair braiding, but the list could have gone on and on. In each case, the method is the same: Usually under the guise of "consumer protection," the government prevents entry by some firms into a market, thereby reducing supply in that market. The effect is much the same as that produced by a fully enforced cartel. Firms thus protected by the government enjoy both a higher price for their product and a larger market share. Consumers—supposedly "protected" by their government—are usually the big losers, due to higher product prices and reduced selection among suppliers.

In Chapter 18, "Education and Choice," we examine what happens when the government has a monopoly over production, where the output produced in this case is education in public schools. There is growing evidence that the quality of education produced by our school system has been declining over the past thirty years, and that a principal reason for this is the government's effective monopoly in the provision of primary and secondary education. One solution to this problem would be to turn primary and secondary education over to the private sector, perhaps accompanied by government-provided education vouchers that low- and middle-income families could use to finance the education they want for their children. Realistically, this solution is probably not politically viable, so this chapter examines another alternative: forcing public schools to compete with one another by permitting children to go to whichever public schools they choose. Based on the evidence from those areas of the country that have experimented with such an arrangement, it appears that the likely result would be a marked improvement in the quality of primary and secondary education in the United States, with *no* increase in spending required to achieve it. It seems that competition works wonders in government, just as it does in the private sector.

15

The E-Commerce Explosion

You can't miss it. It's in the air; it's everywhere. It's the Internet, and hundreds of companies whose names start with a lowercase e or i, or end with dot-com, are changing the way we view the world. The biggest growth area in the new on-line world appears to be **e-commerce**. The latest holiday season was the biggest ever on the Internet. The growth in sales generated through the Internet are estimated to be anywhere from 20 to 50 percent annually. Now, this actually doesn't mean that much, because even in five years retail on-line sales will still be a small fraction of total retail sales in America and an even smaller fraction of retail sales in the world. Still, it is a substantial beginning to what many predict will be a revolution.

Indeed, the business-to-business aspect of e-commerce may become dramatically more important during the same time frame. Automobile manufacturers already do or soon will require that all parts ordering be done on-line. Some of the major companies that provide the infrastructure for the Internet, such as Cisco, already do or soon will require that all ordering be done on-line. The benefits to individual companies and to the economy as a whole center around increased efficiency. Fewer resources will go into the mundane activities associated with buying and selling the intermediate goods that go into manufacturing the final products that we buy as consumers.

Increased economic efficiency may also arise from the growing use of popular on-line auction sites, such as eBay.com and its competitors at Yahoo.com and Amazon.com. (Indeed, if you put "on-line auction" into a search engine such as HotBot, you may find more than 500,000 Web sites to visit.) Auctions have been around for a long time, but never have they been so popular and so accessible.

Traditional supply and demand analysis tells us that the equilibrium price is achieved where the quantity demanded is equal to the quantity supplied. How we get to that equilibrium price is another story. The two most prominent forms of price setting in traditional markets have been one-to-one negotiation and printed price lists. In the former, you haggle with the seller of a good or service, such as in the labor market when you go to various job interviews. In the latter, it's generally a take-it-or-leave-it situation: Sellers present you with prices and you decide whether you want to buy and how much. When a seller sets prices too high, he or she will eventually have to cut those prices to reduce unsold inventory.

Enter the on-line auction. For example, eBay has almost 2000 categories with up to 3 million items for sale at any point in time. The over 4 million members of the so-called eBay community are participating in a new way to make markets more efficient. All on-line shopping presumably reduces the opportunity cost of visiting numerous stores to discover product availability and the best prices. The on-line auction, though, goes one step further: The more buyers and sellers there are on an auction site, the greater your chance of getting a better deal. The reason for this is that the market becomes more liquid; that is, it's easier to find someone who will offer you a favorable price. This is not necessarily true for straight on-line stores, such as BarnesandNoble.com.

On-line auctions do face problems that most off-line stores have already solved. One of them is fraud. A typical retailer will rarely, if ever, engage in fraud with its customers because, in addition to punishing the seller by informing friends and withholding future patronage, customers can readily seek redress from a government agency or through the courts. In contrast, an occasional seller of an item on an eBay auction might fraudulently describe the product being offered or not deliver it, knowing that he or she will likely have no future business to lose in the event the buyer is displeased. Happily for on-line auction participants, the on-line auctioneers and the community of on-line buyers and sellers are solving this potentially serious problem. Regular sellers on eBay and other auction sites establish reputations for being honest and for having reliable delivery. On-line auctioneers facilitate this process by rating sellers based on customer experiences, and publishing buyer comments about sellers.

The world of fixed printed prices is not going to disappear, no matter how popular on-line auctions become. Participating in an on-line auction is not free. Trading on-line involves a time cost and therefore an opportunity cost. It appears that in terms of dollar volume, business-to-business on-line auctions will constitute the lion's share of on-line commercial activity, because time costs are small relative to the volume of business involved in any given transaction. There are even business-to-business auctions that resemble the New York Stock Exchange. One example is e-STEEL, in which many buyers and sellers of steel are brought together. Buyers submit prices they are willing to pay and sellers submit prices at which they are willing to sell. Whenever a match takes place, a transaction occurs.

To some extent, this is the theory underlying the increasingly popular on-line sites where you can offer the maximum amount you are willing to pay for an airline trip or a hotel, for example. Participating sellers of these services then specify the conditions under which they will accept your "bid." If you agree to the terms they specify for your bid, you've got a deal.

One thing is certain: Price comparisons for just about anything seem to be much quicker on-line than off-line. Does this mean that the economy will tend toward perfect information, and therefore less price dispersion? One might think so, but so far no studies have shown this to be true. While on-line retailers tend to be cheaper than their brick-and-mortar rivals, the spread between the highest and lowest prices for a given good is typically as large off-line as on-line. Moreover, it does not seem that on-line retailers with the lowest prices have the largest volume of sales. One study showed that the price for identical books and CDs at different on-line sites differed by as much as 50 percent, with the average being 33 percent for books and 25 percent for CDs.[1]

---

[1] "Understanding Digital Markets: Review and Assessment," July 1999 at http:// ecommerce.mit.edu/paper/ude.

Part of the reason for the continuing price dispersion on the Internet is that so-called intelligent buying agents ("bots") are not yet widely used or perfected. Another reason is the huge variety of sources for on-line purchases. If you go to a typical search engine and put in the words "books" you get thousands of potential Web pages. Perhaps on-line shoppers simply give up and rationally choose to go to Amazon.com or some other well-known site, sacrificing potentially lower prices elsewhere for the convenience of a known site. This is a rational decision if the opportunity cost of the time necessary to search for a lower price is greater than the expected potential cost savings.

Price dispersion on-line may eventually become much less than it is off-line, but there is at least one thing we do know for sure: On-line auctions such as eBay make getting rid of unwanted Christmas gifts easier than ever. Right after Christmas of 1999, eBay became a magnet for unwanted Christmas gifts. This was particularly important for those who received presents that they could not return because they did not know where the gifts were purchased, or had received gifts purchased in other cities, or did not have receipts. As most retailers prepared for the January 2000 slowdown, on-line auction houses were actually gearing up for an increase in business.

eBay executives had in fact noticed an increase in activity after Christmas starting back in 1996. The fact that no one in the public was informed was understandable. eBay kept quiet about the phenomenon for four years because, according to Steve Westly, eBay Senior Vice President, "We try to be sensitive here. No one wants to see a special gift resold." Even on-line, it seems, there are times when ignorance is bliss.

DISCUSSION QUESTIONS

1. What goods would you expect to be the first to be successfully marketed on-line?

2. Why do the operators of on-line auction services publish buyer comments about sellers and customer ratings of sellers? How are they like on-line companies such as bizrate.com that do nothing but rate on-line companies?

3. Are rating services more or less important for on-line companies than for traditional brick-and-mortar firms?

4. What impact will automated search agents ("bots") have on price dispersion on-line? Will this make buyers and sellers better or worse off? Will bots improve or reduce economic efficiency?

16

Pity the Poor Monopolist

A typical explanation of why a monopoly is bad often revolves around price. By definition a monopolist restricts output and thus is able to raise the price above what it otherwise would be. Strange, it might seem then, that in the world of software, computers, and the Internet—where virtually everything gets cheaper every year if not every month—the U.S. Department of Justice successfully prosecuted the Microsoft Corporation for being a monopolist.

In commenting on the decision in the Microsoft case, Connecticut Attorney General Richard Blumenthal stated: "The judge's findings present a compelling picture of a powerful predator abusing its market dominance—an 800-pound gorilla crushing competition and stifling innovation. The three core findings are: Microsoft has a monopoly; it has abused that monopoly; and consumers have been harmed in an 'immediate and easily discernible way.'"

But, say some critics of the decision against Microsoft, virtually all of the products the company sells have fallen in price, so how can consumers have been harmed? When one Justice Department official had this pointed out to him, he stated that the Justice Department has to look to the future. In other words, the Justice Department believes that it knows what the future will bring in the computer industry and that is why it brought suit against the company.

One might say that the Justice Department has been "gunning" for Microsoft for a number of years. A few years ago, the

Justice Department prevented the company from purchasing Intuit, a software firm whose Quicken Home Accounting program was being used by 7 million households. The Justice Department argued then that the merger of one "dominant" market player with another would result in monopoly. Thwarted, Microsoft developed its own competing Money Home Accounting program.

Not too much later, Microsoft became engaged in a pitched battle for leadership in the Internet browser market. Its main competitor was Netscape, which owned the Navigator browser. When Microsoft proposed to bundle the latest version of its own browser, Internet Explorer, with the latest version of its industry-leading Windows operating system and any future improvements on that system, the Justice Department balked. Yet what Microsoft was proposing to do was consistent with what had happened in the software industry for years. Microsoft, Apple, IBM, Sun, Novell, and others have little by little included more features in each operating system they have offered. These integrated features have included graphical user interfaces, type fonts, file compression, networking, and memory management. This same integration also has been observed with virtually all application programs, such as the word processing programs Microsoft Word and Corel WordPerfect. More and more features have been bundled with each new release of the programs.

The Justice Department argued that Microsoft should be compelled to unbundle its Internet browser program from its operating system. The judge in the case cited Supreme Court rulings in other industries and declared that the issues in the Microsoft case were simply ones of old-fashioned market power—its use and its potential abuse. The court stated that "Microsoft's 'unfettered liberty' to impose its idea of what has been 'integrated' into its operating system stops at least at the point at which it would violate established antitrust law." The idea, of course, is that because Microsoft's Windows operating system was used on more than 80 percent of the world's personal computers, bundling forced computer manufacturers who licensed that system to also include the Microsoft Internet Explorer Web browser, causing Netscape and other potential competitors in the browser market to suffer.

During the major antitrust trial against Microsoft in 1999, though, Netscape was purchased by America OnLine (AOL). And less than a year later, AOL announced that it was merging with TimeWarner, one of the world's leading content providers. At the same time that the Justice Department was worried about Microsoft's ability to "crush" its rivals, it appears that those rivals were gearing up to do just that to Microsoft.

Microsoft is not the only successful computer company to incur the wrath of the Justice Department. Not that many years ago, the Justice Department sued IBM for surprisingly similar (in theory, not in detail) antitrust violations. For 19 years (yes, *nineteen* years) the battle waged in the courts. One reason the suit lasted so long is that the Justice Department never defined exactly why it had brought the suit. In the end, the Justice Department asked the court to dismiss its suit against IBM as "without merit." By the time this occurred, IBM was a mere shadow of its former self. Indeed, developments in the rapidly changing personal computer world almost forced IBM to break up into smaller, more profitable companies.

Microsoft is already in somewhat the same situation. Indeed, during the trial, the Justice Department used the term "currently dominant firm." As already noted, however, AOL is challenging Microsoft in many ways. Its acquisitions and mergers program is only one tactic. AOL has outperformed Microsoft in terms of Internet access customers by a ratio of 20 to 1, and this after every computer in the world seemed to have the Microsoft Network System (MNS) Internet access program pre-installed. Sun Microsystems has come after Microsoft by offering a free business suite of applications downloadable from the Internet. On another front, the top ten Internet sites, including Yahoo!, use Oracle database software rather than the one sold by Microsoft. More recently, the free Linux operating system is starting to make inroads against Microsoft's operating system. Even Microsoft's most vocal competitor, Scott McNealy, head of Sun Microsystems, who testified extensively at the antitrust trial, conceded that Microsoft's Windows operating system will only have 50 percent of the market by 2002.

After the antitrust trial, the U.S. Justice Department was faced with the problem of deciding what to do. In traditional antitrust cases, a successful government prosecutor could break up the convicted monopolist into smaller, supposedly more competitive rivals. How this might work in the software and Internet world is hard to assess. After all, despite what the Justice Department thinks, no one really knows where the industry is going and what it will look like in the next few years, let alone in five or ten years. Even Bill Gates correctly pointed out that no great firms have successfully stayed on top during a shift to a new paradigm. Gates almost missed the Internet paradigm, stating only a few years ago that the future would always be in the PC. Even with Gates's decision to step down from CEO to chief software architect at Microsoft, will his company be able to stay on top during the movement away from PCs to networking, the Internet, and who knows what else? Certainly the Justice Department is in no better position to answer this question than anyone else.

DISCUSSION QUESTIONS

1. The word *monopoly* is from Latin and literally means "single seller." How is it true that every firm is a monopoly if we take this word literally? If we are not quite so literal, and recognize that all goods have substitutes, how is it true that no firm, not even Microsoft, is a "monopoly"?

2. Presumably, the judge in the Microsoft case did not have in mind either of the extremes mentioned in question 1. What do you suppose he did have in mind? That is, what "wrong" was he trying to right by his decision? What, then, should we see happen as a result of the Microsoft decision?

3. A counterargument to the Justice Department's position is that Microsoft rose to its position of market leadership by doing a better job than other firms of providing customers with what they want. If this argument is correct, what should happen as a result of the Microsoft decision?

4. Microsoft's competitors apparently played a key role in convincing the Justice Department to bring the suit and providing important testimony against Microsoft during the trial. Why do you think they did this? Does your answer shed any light on what will likely happen as a result of the judge's decision in this case?

17

Keeping the
Competition Out

Most competitors hate competition. And who can blame them? After all, if a firm can keep the competition out, profits are sure to rise. How high they will rise obviously varies by industry, but the lowly taxicab market gives some indication of what is at stake. In New York City, the number of taxicabs is limited by law—limited, in fact, to 12,187 cabs in a city of 8 million people. (That's about one cab for every 650 people, in a town where many people don't own cars.) To legally operate a taxi in New York, one must own a taxi medallion, a city-issued metal shield affixed to a cab's hood. After capping the number of medallions since 1937, the city offered 133 new ones for sale in 1996. Winning bidders paid about $175,000 for each medallion—that is, for the right to work seventy-hour weeks, subject to robbery, rude customers, and the erratic driving habits of other cabbies. And lest you think New York taxi drivers are crazy to pay such sums, keep this in mind: Because the city keeps the competition out, the taxi business is so lucrative that the medallions can be used as collateral to borrow money at favorable interest rates, and any cabby who wants to leave the business can immediately find a buyer for his medallion, usually at a price that will bring even more profit. And those new medallions that went for $175,000 in 1996? Well, by 2000 they were worth $250,000.

Keeping the competition out works this way: Reducing the number of firms in an industry decreases the supply of the good, thus driving up its price. Firms that remain thereby enjoy both a higher price for their product and a larger market share. Consumers lose, however, suffering not only from higher prices but also from fewer alternative sources of supply from which to choose. Another group of losers is comprised of the firms who are excluded. They are forced to go into lower-paying pursuits for which they are not as well suited. The higher profits enjoyed by the firms who are protected from competition thus come at the expense of consumers and excluded competitors; the net result is also an overall loss to society as a whole, because the limit on competition reduces the total extent of mutually beneficial exchange.

Note we said that the number of taxi medallions in New York is limited by the government. This is typical. Even though many government agencies (for example, the Federal Trade Commission and the Department of Justice at the federal level) are supposed to promote competition, the most effective way to *prevent* competition is usually to get the government involved. Consider telephones. It used to be that both long-distance and local telephone markets were regulated by the federal government. In 1984 the long-distance market was deregulated, and AT&T had to begin competing with MCI and Sprint for customers. The result was a 40 percent drop in inflation-adjusted long-distance rates. Local telephone service continued to be regulated by the Federal Communications Commission (FCC), however, and over the same period of time, local phone rates have *risen* 40 percent in real terms—chiefly because the FCC has kept competition out of the local phone service market.

The government of Mexico has been even more successful in protecting phone giant Telmex from competition. Formerly a state-owned company, Telmex was privatized in 1990, with the understanding that the government would gradually but steadily end the firm's monopoly. The thought was nice, but the monopoly remains. Telmex has effectively been permitted to prevent potential entrants to the Mexican phone market from connecting through its dominant switching equipment. The result has been sky-high connection charges and virtually no new connections. Hence, there are now only 10 telephones per 100 inhabitants of Mexico. In Poland, the fellow member of the Organization of Economic Cooperation and Development with the next fewest number of lines, there are 20 telephones per 100 inhabitants. In addition to poor service, the lack of competition also shows up in prices, which sharply hampers Mexican businesses. For example, a U.S. firm trying to drum up business in London would pay $5.40 to make five phone calls to Britain of four minutes each. Those same calls would cost its Mexican rival $25.40.

Many of the decision makers who work for the government agencies that limit competition are lawyers, so it is not surprising that competition among lawyers is limited. For example, in every state but one (California), the number of law schools is capped by state law, thereby restricting entry into the profession and driving up earnings. The high fees lawyers earn have in turn generated competition from lawyers' assistants, called *paralegals*. This competition—or rather, attempted competition—can be seen in the market for personal bankruptcies. Rising consumer debt, combined with less restrictive federal bankruptcy law, has produced a massive increase in personal bankruptcies. Over the past decade, the number of people declaring bankruptcy has grown to 1 million per year, up from 400,000 per year. A typical personal bankruptcy case costs about $750 when done by a lawyer, but the procedure is a simple one, requiring only that some standard paperwork be filled out and filed with the relevant authorities. Thus in come the paralegals (who, if working for a lawyer, would be doing the paperwork anyway), offering to perform the same services for, say, $269. Faced with competition like this, the legal profession struck back, gaining passage of Section 110 of the Bankruptcy Reform Act. This statute gives judges the power to cap the fees paralegals can charge. Thus far, imposed caps have run from $50 to $100 per case, which is low enough to force most paralegals out. Paralegals who charge more than the legal limit are subject to fines of up to $500 for each violation of the law. Lawyers are free to charge what they like, sometimes as much as $1500, now that they don't have paralegals to worry about.

Sometimes the government gets involved in some unlikely markets in its efforts to prevent the ravages of competition from taking their toll. Consider hair-braiding. Some African Americans like to have their hair straightened in beauty shops, a procedure that requires a touch-up every four weeks, for an average monthly cost (excluding cutting and styling) of about $100. An alternative is to get one's hair braided at a braiding salon. There are now about 10,000 of these salons across the country, and they are growing in popularity. Braids need maintenance only once every ten weeks, cutting the cost to $50 per month. The same low cost and convenience that make braiding salons attractive to consumers also make them threatening to the conventional beauty shops that straighten hair, especially in fashion-conscious California. Claiming that they are seeking to protect consumers, agents of the California Barbering & Cosmetology Board have begun raiding the salons of unlicensed hair braiders. Not surprisingly, the hair braiders think the state is actually trying to protect state-licensed cosmetologists at beauty shops, who must spend $6000 for 1600 hours of training to get their licenses. Indeed, one of the braiders, Ali Rasheed, argues that the marketplace is better than state licensing boards at protecting consumers. "It's simple," he says. "If I mess up your hair, you don't come back. You spread the word. And very quickly I'd be out of business." Perhaps so, but it looks like the state of California doesn't want to give consumers that option.

Apparently, the government doesn't like competition, either. The U.S. Postal Service, a federal government corporation, faces potential competition from Federal Express, a privately owned express delivery company. Although the Postal Service has been unable to prevent FedEx from making considerable inroads on its parcel delivery service, it has had more luck in keeping FedEx out of the first-class mail business, by getting the U.S. Congress to mandate that anyone wishing to have a letter delivered by FedEx must affix postage stamps in addition to paying the FedEx delivery rates!

Back in New York, there is yet another example of the fact that the government likes to protect itself from competition. New York City is well known for its massive public transit system, comprising both subways and bus lines. What is not so well known is that mass transit in New York City started off as private enterprise. The first horsecars and elevated trains in the city were developed by private companies. Moreover, even though New York's first subway was partly financed by a loan from the city, it was otherwise a private operation, operated profitably at a fare of a nickel (the equivalent of less than a dollar today).

New York's politicians refused to allow fares to rise during the inflation of World War I, yielding financial losses for the private transit companies. Promising to show the private sector how to run a transit system efficiently, while simultaneously offering to protect the public from the "dictatorship" of the transit firms, the city took over the subway, merged it with the bus line, and promptly started raising fares. Despite fare increases double the inflation rate, however, costs have risen even faster, so that today, even though the basic fare is $1.50, the city *loses* $2 a passenger.

Enter the jitneys, privately owned vans that operate along regular routes, like buses, but which charge only a $1 a passenger and will make detours for pick-ups and drop-offs on request. Actually, we should have said "attempted entry" by the jitneys, because the New York City Council—at the insistence of the public transit system—has denied operating permits to almost all jitney operators who have applied. The Council says it is only seeking to prevent the vans from causing accidents and traffic problems, but even fully insured drivers who have met federal requirements for operating interstate van services are routinely denied permits. Thus most of the hundreds of jitneys operating in New York City do so illegally. Even the few jitneys that have managed to get licensed are forbidden from operating along public bus routes—all in the name of public safety, of course.

Transportation economists such as Daniel Klein of Santa Clara University have argued that public transit systems could once more be profitable—instead of losing sixty cents on the dollar—if the jitneys were given a chance. "Government has demonstrated that it has no more business producing transit than producing cornflakes. It should concentrate instead on establishing new rules to foster competition," says Klein. Unfortunately for the jitneys and their customers, however, that competition would come at the expense of New York's public transit system. Thus, for the foreseeable future, it seems the jitneys will have to compete only by breaking the laws, because like most competitors, the New York City mass transit system just hates competition.

DISCUSSION QUESTIONS

1. If you were operating a business, would you encourage competitors to start operating in your market? Would you attempt to use legal means to prevent them from competing with you?

2. Consider two different ways of beating your competition. One is to offer your customers lower prices and better service. The other is to get a law passed that raises your competitors' costs—for example, by imposing special operating requirements on them. Can you see any difference between these two, assuming that both succeed in keeping your competition out?

3. Although governments at all levels sometimes act to prevent some individuals from competing with others, the federal government is probably the most active in this role, state governments are less active, and local governments are the least active. Can you explain this pattern?

4. Is there any difference between prohibiting entry by a group of firms and levying a special tax on those firms?

18

Education and Choice

In 1974, East Harlem ranked thirty-second among New York City's thirty-two community school districts. Only 15 percent of its students read at or above grade level. By 1989 this inner-city school district ranked sixteenth, and more than 65 percent of its students read at or above grade level. By the late 1990s, the East Harlem district—located in one of the poorest areas of New York—was still improving and had a *waiting list* of teachers wishing to work there. What happened in East Harlem? A massive infusion of federal funds to promote educational reform? A multi-year grant from a major charitable foundation? Perhaps an influx of upscale, yuppie parents demanding educational excellence? The answer: none of the above. What happened in East Harlem can be summarized by just one word: *choice.*

In 1974 the administrators of the East Harlem school district, faced with a school system that had nowhere to go but up, made a radical move: They decided to permit choice in their district. Teachers and schools were permitted to choose curricula and programs they thought would provide the best educational products, and students and parents were allowed to choose from among those products the ones best suited to their preferences and educational objectives. Along the way, mistakes were made and lessons learned. Some schools did a poor job, failed to attract new customers, and have closed their doors. Other schools provided popular, effective programs that have been replicated successfully elsewhere in the district. Overall, the quality of education in East Harlem improved beyond even the most optimistic expectations of 1974. Indeed, the improvement was so great that the East Harlem educators decided to enter a new market. The district had been administering education through the eighth grade only; in 1985 it assumed responsibility for a neighborhood high school with a graduation rate of 7 percent. Although the school accepts any student who wants to attend, its graduation rate now exceeds 90 percent, and almost all of its graduates go on to some kind of postsecondary education.

The freedom of choice offered schools, teachers, parents, and students in the East Harlem school district is unusual in public school systems today, but so is the success of East Harlem schools. In most school districts, the curriculum and course offerings for each grade level are decided on from "on high"—at the level of the district or the state administrator. Once it is decided that chemistry and biology but not geology are to be offered in high schools, all high schools in the district typically must abide by that decision. Moreover, all individuals teaching chemistry generally must follow the approved study plan and use the approved book for that course without regard for the talents or interests of the particular teachers. The choices available to the consumers of education—students and their parents—are equally circumscribed. Once they have chosen a place to live, they are stuck with the particular set of schools, elementary through secondary, to which they are assigned by the district. If high school A offers advanced placement chemistry and high school B does not, then students assigned to high school B simply will not have the option of taking advanced placement chemistry in the public school system.

In important respects, then, each school district and each school within a district is much like a monopolist, albeit on a small scale. If the customers (students and their parents) of a district are dissatisfied with the quality, type, or amount of product being offered, they cannot—short of physically moving—choose to consume the services of another public school district. Similarly, if students or parents are dissatisfied with their assigned school within a district, they cannot choose a competing public school within the district.

Parents and students can attempt to alter district or school policies by writing letters, voicing their opinions in school board or PTA meetings, or engaging in political activities. Yet if they are in the minority by even one vote, they are stuck with the preferences of the majority. It is also true that people can "vote with their feet" by relocating their residences to another school district or by utilizing the services of private schools. Such measures, however, are very costly and generally are taken only by persons who are either extremely dissatisfied or extremely wealthy. Few people are willing to sustain the cost and inconvenience of selling one house and buying another simply to enjoy a school system that is a little better—particularly because they will have so little voice in the operation of the new school system once they have chosen it. For those people opting for private schools, there is a double burden to bear: In addition to the bills for private school tuition, they must continue paying taxes to support the public school system they find unsatisfactory! All in all, public schools are largely insulated from competition.

This situation is in sharp contrast to the market for magazines, for example; like schools, magazines are a source of knowledge and (for some) entertainment. Consider *Time* magazine, which is headquartered in Manhattan, a borough of New York City. Taxes are not levied on the residents of Manhattan to cover the costs of publishing *Time*, and one need not be a resident of Manhattan to read it; residents of Brooklyn, East Harlem, and even Honolulu are free to read it should they choose to pay for it. If the owners of *Time* produce a high-quality product at a reasonable price, readership will grow and the owners of the magazine will become wealthy (presumably the reason the owners are in business). If the owners produce a shoddy product or charge a price that is too high, consumers can switch to any of numerous competing newsmagazines, thereby reducing the wealth of the owners of *Time*. In either event, competition among magazines yields diversity of choice and the provision of high-quality products at reasonable prices.

We have already noted how the relative lack of competition among public schools restricts the choices available to parents and students. Many experts also believe that the monopolistic position of public schools has contributed to inferior primary and secondary education in the United States relative to other comparable nations and to a significant decline in educational quality in the United States over the past quarter-century.

It has long been recognized that when U.S. students are exposed to educational systems in other industrialized nations, they are commonly at least a grade level behind the other students in those countries, even in standard subjects such as mathematics.

Recent research has systematically confirmed this observation. One major study found that the *average* Japanese student outscores the top 5 percent of U.S. students enrolled in college-prep math courses. Other research has revealed that in chemistry and physics, advanced science students in U.S. high schools perform worse than their counterparts in almost all countries studied. In biology, U.S. students ranked dead last, behind such nations as Singapore and Thailand.

The superior performance of foreign high school students can be explained in part by the fact that many foreign nations place more emphasis on training at the primary and secondary school levels and less emphasis on college-level training. Nevertheless, it is telling that competition is the rule among school systems in most other developed nations. The French, for example, have two parallel systems above the elementary grades, a public one and a Catholic one, both paid for out of taxes. The Italian system is similar. In Japan, schools are graded by the performance of their students on the university entrance exams, and teachers in high-ranking schools are promoted and paid accordingly. Many observers agree the lack of competitive pressure among public school systems in this country has largely robbed U.S. schools of the incentive to excel. Even the president of the American Federation of Teachers acknowledged the deficiency in U.S. schools: "Only about 5 percent of our graduates leave high school prepared to do what is considered real college-level work. . . . The overwhelming majority of American students who go on to higher education will be learning in college what their European colleagues learned in high school or even junior high school."

There is little doubt that the quality of education in American school systems has deteriorated over the past quarter-century. Between 1963 and 1980, scores on the widely used Scholastic Aptitude Test (SAT) plunged ninety points; by 2000 they had recovered only about twenty points of that loss. Between 1972 and 1981 the number of high school seniors scoring above 600 (out of a possible 800) on the verbal portion of the SAT dropped 40 percent; by 2000 this remained 25 percent below the 1972 figure. Although scores on the mathematics portion of the SAT have held up somewhat better, this amounts to little more than stagnation in an area requiring significant improvement. A few years ago, the federally funded National Assessment of Educational Progress

(NAEP) found that, despite supposed efforts at educational reform in this country, the previous decade had witnessed improvements in mathematics skills that were "confined primarily to lower order skills." Indeed, the NAEP report concluded that only 6.4 percent of high school seniors have mastered "multi-step problem solving and algebra"—exactly the sort of skills essential to successful performance at the college level.[1]

What can be done about the sad state of primary and secondary education in this country? Many observers argue that competition among schools, fostered by greater freedom of choice, is essential to any solution. The experiment of the East Harlem school district is one example of the power of choice in promoting excellence. On a much broader scale, a series of programs in the state of Minnesota are providing even more compelling evidence of the importance of choice.

Several years ago, the governor of Minnesota proposed that juniors and seniors in public schools in the state be permitted to receive all or part of their last two years of high school in colleges or vocational schools, with state monies following them from high school to pay their tuition, lab fees, and book fees. The governor also recommended that families be allowed to send their children to public schools outside their home districts, as long as the receiving districts had room and the movement did not harm desegregation efforts. Despite vigorous opposition to the proposals by the teachers' unions, school boards, and superintendents' groups, four laws allowing greater freedom of educational choice have been passed in Minnesota, and the results are encouraging.

In the first five years of its operation, more than 10,000 students took advantage of the program permitting them to take college courses while still in high school, and many of them had higher grade point averages in those courses than the first-year college students. The program has attracted hundreds of students who had dropped out of high school due to boredom or frustration. Many participants are the first in their families to attend college. As one of

---

[1] Consider, for example, the following question: "Which of the following is true of 87 percent of 10? (a) It is greater than 10. (b) It is less than 10. (c) It is equal to 10. (d) Can't tell?" The NAEP report concluded that all high school seniors should be able to answer this question correctly. In fact, only 51 percent were able to do so.

these students put it, the program "changed my sense of what was possible."

Just as important, the program has stimulated many high schools to improve their own programs. For example, the number of advanced placement courses offered by Minnesota high schools quadrupled—without any new mandates or dollars targeted for this purpose. Dozens of high schools have been encouraged to establish cooperative programs with colleges and universities that let them offer courses right in the high schools.

Under another Minnesota program, students who do not succeed in one junior or senior high school are allowed to attend a school outside their district. Several thousand students have already taken advantage of this plan, about half of them school dropouts. Another law enables Minnesota students in all grades to attend school outside their districts, subject to space and racial balance considerations. By 2000, a modest but significant proportion of students each year were exercising their right to choose among public schools in Minnesota.

There is also a growing movement across the country that seeks to expand the use of charter schools. These are publicly funded but privately operated schools that receive operating charters from local school districts or the state government where they are located. Although the schools receive public money, parents and friends of the charter schools are basically responsible for recruiting teachers, finding classroom facilities, and all other aspects of school operation. In return, however, they are given great latitude in designing curricula that meet the desires of the students and their parents. Although there still are only about 200,000 students attending charter schools nationwide, many advocates of educational choice regard them as being a major potential source of competition for regular public schools over the next decade.

In a slightly different vein, in 1996 the city of Cleveland, Ohio, began a state-funded program of scholarships that could be used to attend private schools. The scholarships were awarded to 1,996 low-income children in grades kindergarten through three. Each scholarship, or **voucher**, covered up to 90 percent of the private school's tuition, up to a maximum of $2,500 (about one-third the annual per-pupil cost of Cleveland public schools). At the end of the program's first year of operation, Harvard University evaluated the program and came to two key conclusions. First, the children in the program showed significant improvement in their academic performance in both reading and mathematics. Second, their parents were far more satisfied with their schools' performance than were the parents of children still in public schools. And this was true whether the parents were asked about academic quality, school safety, discipline, or any of the other indicators surveyed. Overall satisfaction was 71 percent for parents of children in the scholarship program, compared to 25 percent for parents of children in the public school system.

By 1999, many of the 3500 students that were then enrolled in the program were using the vouchers to attend religious schools. This had produced a legal challenge to the system, based on the argument that public funds were being used unconstitutionally to fund religious institutions. This issue may prove to be a fundamental impediment to the use of vouchers as a means of promoting educational choice.

The East Harlem and Minnesota programs show that when choice among schools is permitted, the resulting competition improves the quality of education. Over the last few years, at least seven other states have followed Minnesota's lead, offering their students the option of attending school in a different district. The Cleveland program, which has been implemented in slightly modified form in both Milwaukee and New York City, illustrates that it is possible to successfully promote choice not merely between different public schools but also between public and private schools. Programs in these and other locales are reaffirming this conclusion: When students are given a choice of schools, graduation rates improve, student achievement increases, and parents are more involved and satisfied. Even teachers and administrators—often initially fearful of the consequences of competition—are finding that the opportunity to create new and distinctive programs offers rewards far outweighing the extra effort involved.

The famous golfer Arnold Palmer once remarked, "If you're not competing, you're dead." For America's moribund public school systems, the message from Minnesota, East Harlem, and elsewhere seems to be the converse: Competition brings vitality. It is easy to imagine that today's students are hoping this message is being received as clearly as it is being transmitted.

DISCUSSION QUESTIONS

1. Who gains and who loses when there is more competition among public schools?

2. Some people have argued that we should institute educational vouchers (like those tried in Cleveland) that could be used by students to finance their education in either public schools or private schools of their choice. What are the advantages and disadvantages of such a scheme?

3. Why is most schooling in the United States operated by governments and paid for by taxpayers, rather than being privately provided and financed? Does your answer imply that most medical care, for example, should be provided by the government and paid for by taxpayers? Answer the same question regarding food, clothing, and shelter.

4. In general, most state universities charge lower tuition to in-state students than to out-of-state students. The implicit subsidy to in-state students averages about $5000 per school year, but students may only take advantage of the subsidy if they stay in their home state—they cannot take a $5000 voucher with them to use at a college in another state. What would happen to competition among colleges if students could take their subsidies to whatever state they preferred? What is likely to happen to the quality of college education? Would you go to your state university if you could take your subsidy wherever you liked?

Part Five

Political Economy

INTRODUCTION

The chief focus of economics has always been on explaining the behavior of the private sector. Yet dating back at least to the publication of Adam Smith's *Wealth of Nations* more than 200 years ago, economists have never missed an opportunity to apply their theories to additional realms of behavior. For the past thirty years or so, much of this effort has been devoted to developing theories that explain the actions of governments, as well as the consequences of those actions. This undertaking is often referred to as the study of political economy, for it often involves a mixture of politics and economics. As the selections in this section hint, economists do not yet have a unified theory of government. Nevertheless, they are making progress and are sometimes able to offer surprising insights.

One of the first things that economists had to learn about government decision making is that the costs of government policies are always higher than promised, and the benefits are always lower. This simple proposition forms the centerpiece of Chapter 19, "Killer Cars and the Rise of the SUV," which explores the implications of federal rules that specify the minimum fuel efficiency permitted for new cars sold in the United States. Sometimes the effects of the federal regulations are surprisingly pervasive—as they are when they induce one-third of American drivers to switch from cars to trucks in response to federal fuel economy rules. Sometimes the effects are at least moderately expensive—as they are when they induce companies to spend millions of dollars redesigning vehicles, not to make them more fuel efficient but solely to satisfy the peculiar accounting conventions of the regulations. And sadly, sometimes the effects of the regulations are tragic: Indeed, reliable estimates suggest that the federal fuel economy standards have forced automakers to downsize their cars to such an extent as to make them less crashworthy. It is estimated that 3000 Americans lose their lives in traffic accidents every year as a result of these particular regulations.

Many government regulatory programs are supposed to protect lives. For example, the federal Superfund program was implemented in 1980 with the avowed goal of protecting Americans from the hazards of toxic wastes. It was supposed to be a short-lived, speedy program to rid the nation of dangerous waste disposal sites, such as the notorious Love Canal in New York. It was to cost at most a few billion dollars, paid for by those firms whose pollution had posed the risks or caused the harms. *Not one* of these goals has been achieved: As we see in Chapter 20, "Superfund Follies," cleanup is slow, costs are astronomical, and much of the program's resources are diverted to activities that do little good. How could such a well intentioned program turn out to be such a "disaster" as one U.S. president has termed it? Perhaps not surprisingly, the answer is politics, and so the Superfund program is a fascinating, albeit sad, example of political economy in action.

Crime rates that have gone up hand-in-hand with prison populations, coupled with criminals who seem impervious to law enforcement, have led many people to ask a simple if disturbing question: Is there *any* effective way to fight crime? Although economic theory says the answer to this question is "yes," the empirical estimates obtained by economists have said, well, "maybe." Yet as we see in Chapter 21, "Crime and Punishment," new evidence is shedding light on the answer to this question. Indeed, it is increasingly clear that the two central tools of traditional law enforcement—police to apprehend the criminals and prisons to punish them—may be every bit as effective as their proponents claim in discouraging criminal activity. Two lessons that emerge from this chapter are that politicians are likely to continue pouring more money into law enforcement, and those resources are going to have a growing impact in reducing crime in America.

For thirty years America struggled with the baby-boom generation as it graduated from bassinets to BMWs. For the next thirty years, we shall have to grapple with the problems that arise as the boomers progress from corporate boardrooms to nursing homes. As we see in Chapter 22, "The Graying of America," our nation is aging at the fastest rate in our history. It will not be long before all of America looks much like Florida, the retirement capital of the world, looks today. As America ages, two major problems in political economy are emerging. First, we must face the issue of paying the Social Security and Medicare bills of the rapidly growing elderly portion of the population. Second, as increasing numbers of people retire, there will be fewer workers capable of bearing the growing tax burden. America must learn new ways of utilizing the productive capabilities of the elderly and accept the fact that—as much as we may wish otherwise—sometimes the elderly may simply have to fend for themselves; otherwise, today's college students will soon find the financial burden beyond their capacity.

19

Killer Cars and the Rise of the SUV

Things are not always what they seem.
—Phaedrus, circa A.D. 8

If there were a Murphy's Law of economic policy making, it would be this: *The costs are always higher than promised, and the benefits are always lower.* The federal law that regulates automobile fuel economy provides just one example of this fundamental principle and along the way demonstrates that what Phaedrus had to say two thousand years ago is true today.

Our story begins in the 1970s, when the United States was in the middle of the so-called energy crisis. The Organization of Petroleum Exporting Countries (OPEC), a cartel of major oil-producing countries, had succeeded in raising the prices of petroleum products (including gasoline) to record-high levels. Consumers reacted by conserving on their use of gasoline and other petroleum products, and Congress responded by enacting legislation mandating energy conservation as the law of the land. One of these laws, known as the corporate average fuel economy (CAFE) standard, requires that each auto manufacturer's passenger cars sold in this country meet a federally mandated fuel economy standard. The new car fleets for the year 2000, for example, had to average 27.5 miles per gallon (mpg) of gasoline. If an automaker sells a gas-guzzler that gets only 15 mpg, somewhere along the line it must also sell enough gas-sipping subcompacts so that the average fuel economy of the entire fleet of cars sold by the company works out to 27.5 mpg. If an automaker's average fuel economy is worse than 27.5 mpg, the corporation is fined $5 per car for each 0.1 mpg it falls short. For example, if General Motors were to fail to meet the CAFE standard by only one mpg, it could be subject to penalties of $200 million per year or more.

The CAFE standard was first introduced at a time when the price of gasoline, measured in terms of today's dollars, was about $3 per gallon. During the mid-1980s, price-cutting by members of the OPEC cartel, combined with a rise in oil production elsewhere, sent gasoline prices into free fall. By 2000, with gasoline less than half as expensive (in inflation-adjusted dollars) as it was in the 1970s, the legally mandated CAFE standard of 27.5 mpg almost certainly resulted in cars that didn't consume *enough* gasoline. This seems like a strange conclusion, so we want to be sure we understand why it is correct.

There is no doubt that conserving gasoline is a good thing, for gasoline is a scarce good. If we are able to accomplish the same objectives (such as making a trip to the grocery store) and use less gasoline in doing so, the money that would have been spent on the gas can now be spent on other goods. Yet conserving gasoline is itself a costly activity. In the extreme case, we could engage in 100 percent conservation of gasoline, but doing so would mean giving up automobiles altogether! Somewhat more realistically, reducing the amount of gasoline that cars burn requires that they be lighter, have smaller engines, and be smaller and sometimes less crash-resistant. To meet the CAFE standards, for example, automobile manufacturers had to switch to production techniques that are more costly, use materials (such as aluminum and high-tech plastics) that are more easily damaged in accidents and more costly to repair, and design engines that are less responsive and more difficult and costly to repair. Although these are all things that probably would make sense if the price of gas were $3 per gallon, many economists believe that at $1.50 per gallon the principal effect of the CAFE standard is to raise consumers' total transportation costs: The costs of conserving on gasoline exceed the savings from consuming less of it.

But the costs of the CAFE standard are measured not just in terms of the dollars and cents of reduced economic efficiency. They are also measured in terms of people whose lives are lost as the result of the law—thousands of lives every year.

The seemingly obvious way to respond to a law that requires enhanced fuel efficiency is to redesign engines so that they burn less fuel. Indeed, the automakers have done exactly this. But another highly effective means of reducing the fuel appetite of automobiles is to downsize them by making them smaller and lighter. A major study by Robert Crandall of the Brookings Institute and John Graham of Harvard found that the CAFE standard forced automakers to produce cars that are about 500 pounds lighter than they would have been without the law. A 500-pound weight reduction implies a 14 percent increase in the fatality risk for the occupants of a car involved in an accident. That translates into approximately 3000 additional deaths per year, plus another 15,000 or so serious nonfatal injuries each year.

Apparently, consumers have not been happy with the lighter and less powerful cars, nor with the higher attendant risk of death they imply. Fortunately, consumers have found a way out: Light trucks, which include vans, pickups, and sport utility vehicles (SUVs) have been subject to a less demanding fuel economy standard. In contrast to the standard for cars, established in 1978 at 18.0 mpg, and now at 27.5 mpg, the CAFE standard for light trucks, initially set in 1980 at 17.5 mpg, is currently 20.6 mpg. Hence, the CAFE standards initially were less stringent for light trucks than for cars, and they have been raised less sharply (up 17.1 percent for light trucks, versus up 52.8 percent for cars).

Frustrated—and safety-conscious—consumers have thus been able to substitute out of passenger cars and thereby escape some of the consequences that Congress otherwise would have inflicted on them. Indeed, according to research by economist Paul E. Godek, CAFE has induced millions of consumers to move away from small cars and into larger, higher-powered SUVs and other light trucks.[1] Between 1975 and 1995, the light-truck share of passenger vehicles rose to 41.5 percent from 20.9 percent. Godek estimates that without CAFE the light-truck share would only have been 29.2 percent. Hence, about three-fifths of the rise in the light-truck market share has been induced by the CAFE standards. By the year 2000, the market share for SUVs and other light trucks had reached fully 50

[1] Paul E. Godek, "The Regulation of Fuel Economy and the Demand for 'Light Trucks.'" *Journal of Law & Economics*, October 1997, pp. 495-509.

percent of the 17 million passenger vehicles sold each year, a remarkable transformation in the market in less than 25 years.

The original goal of CAFE was (in part) to induce substitution from large cars to small ones. But the rise of the SUV has, to some extent, frustrated this intent. Two consequences have resulted. First, light trucks are less fuel-efficient than passenger cars, so fuel economy has risen less than if light-truck substitution had not been possible. A rough estimate of this effect is that it is probably fairly modest—reducing overall fuel economy by about 1.0 mpg.

More important are the consequences in the arena of passenger vehicle safety. Despite their name, light trucks are heavier than cars. Because there are more light trucks on the road with CAFE-lightened cars, drivers of those cars are now at increased risk of death in crashes involving light trucks. This effect has made national headlines from time to time, as people have worried about the adverse effects for the occupants of small cars that tangle with large SUVs.

But there is a second effect. The occupants of light trucks are protected by the very mass that is hazardous to the occupants of cars. This mass not only protects light-truck occupants from cars, it protects them from heavy trucks, trees, wildlife, and so on. This, in turn, tends to cut accident fatalities. Crandall and Graham's earlier work on the impact of vehicle weight on fatality rates suggests that the substitution toward light trucks may actually, on balance, have reduced overall fatalities—meaning that CAFE is not killing quite as many extra people each year as it would without the rise of the SUV.

There remains one mystery in the CAFE story, which is why the law was originally enacted. If the real objective of CAFE was fuel economy (and thus, in part, environmental protection), this could have been accomplished much more cheaply with a direct tax on gasoline. The structure of the law suggests a different congressional motive. CAFE treats domestic and imported cars separately. Manufacturers must meet the standard for both fleets, so they can't simply import fuel-efficient cars to bring up the average mileage of their domestic cars. Instead, they must make more small cars here in America. Thus, CAFE has protected the jobs of domestic auto workers—giving us one more example of a law supposedly enacted to achieve a high-minded goal that instead serves chiefly to insulate a U.S. industry from the rigors of competition.

So, the next time a minivan takes your parking place, or an oversized four-wheeler tailgates you, remember this: Their owners are just trying to prevent Congress from killing them to save jobs in Detroit.

DISCUSSION QUESTIONS

1. Why do you think Congress passed the CAFE standard?

2. Does your answer to question 1 imply either (1) consumers do not know what is in their own best interest, or (2) firms will not voluntarily provide the goods (including fuel economy) consumers want to purchase?

3. Suppose Congress really knows what the best average fuel economy for automobiles is. How do you think "best" is (or should be) defined? Do the costs and benefits of achieving a particular level of fuel economy play a role in determining that definition?

4. If Congress wanted to increase the average fuel economy of cars, could it accomplish this by imposing a tax on gasoline? What are the advantages and disadvantages of using taxes rather than standards to achieve an improvement in fuel economy?

20

Superfund Follies

Superfund has been a disaster.
—William Jefferson Clinton, 1993

In 1978 residents near Love Canal, an abandoned waste site in Niagara Falls, New York, found chemicals leaking into their homes. Fearing that these chemicals might be causing health problems in the neighborhood, the state of New York declared a public health emergency. Ultimately, the government ordered the neighborhood abandoned, and more than 200 houses and a school were bulldozed. Although no scientific study has produced any credible evidence that the chemicals at Love Canal harmed anyone, the episode had one other lasting and very costly result: It induced Congress in 1980 to establish the Superfund program.[1]

Superfund was supposed to be a short-lived, speedy program to rid the nation of dangerous waste disposal sites like Love Canal. It was to cost at most a few billion dollars, paid for by those firms whose pollution had posed the risks or caused the harms. *None* of those intentions have been achieved: Cleanup is slow, costs are astronomical, and much of the program's resources are diverted to activities that do little good.

Despite twenty years of spending, less than 10 percent of the nation's Superfund sites have been cleaned up. This slow pace is not because of any lack of resources: The Environmental Protection

---

[1] The full name of the legislation that created Superfund is the Comprehensive Environmental Response and Liability Act (CERCLA). For more on the history of the program, see Richard L. Stroup, "Superfund: The Shortcut That Failed," *PERC Policy Series PS-5,* 1996.

Agency (EPA), which is charged with administering the Superfund program, is devoting more than a billion taxpayer dollars a year to it. Private firms that are cleaning up sites are spending an additional $1.5 billion per year on this task. By the EPA's own accounting, the agency's overhead costs run about $450 for every hour of work performed by its contractors in cleaning up sites—and this number does not include the wage or overhead costs charged by the cleanup firm. Moreover, of the billions spent each year on Superfund, roughly one-third is squandered on legal and other transaction costs—activities that ultimately clean up nothing.

One estimate of the magnitude of the waste involved in Superfund cleanups is contained in a recent study by economists Kip Viscusi of Harvard and James Hamilton of Duke.[2] They found that EPA cleanups of Superfund sites cost an average of almost $12 billion for every cancer case prevented. Even more amazing is that virtually all—99.5 percent—of the cancer cases that will be averted by EPA efforts are prevented by the first 5 percent of the agency's expenditures. The remaining 95 percent of expenditures prevent only 0.5 percent of the cancer cases—at a cost per case of an astonishing $200 billion.

Cleanup at Superfund sites targets chemical pathways. These are the specific ways in which people are exposed to particular chemicals—such as breathing in contaminated dust or drinking water from a well that has been tainted by a toxic chemical seepage. When the pathways pose a high risk, cleanup is mandatory; cleanup of low-risk pathways is at the discretion of local EPA officials. Viscusi and Hamilton found that the forces pushing the extent of cleanup often vary markedly between these two types of sites. To cite just one example of EPA's inconsistency, in high-risk settings, the agency sets more stringent cleanup standards the greater the population density, a policy that seems sensible enough. But in low-risk settings, greater population density leads the EPA to choose less stringent standards—an outcome that is arguably foolish.

Overall, Viscusi and Hamilton found that "Superfund site [cleanup] decisions do not follow the expected pattern for efficient

[2] W. Kip Viscusi and James T. Hamilton, "Are Risk Regulators Rational? Evidence from Hazardous Waste Cleanup Decisions," *American Economic Review*, September 1999, pp. 1010–1027.

risk management." Because Congress directs the EPA to make Superfund decisions but does not order the agency to consider costs, this is perhaps not surprising. What is disconcerting is the nature of the factors that replace cost-effectiveness in guiding EPA decisions: misplaced risk perceptions and political influence.

For example, a key ingredient in determining EPA cleanup stringency is the public notoriety of the chemicals at the site. Even after controlling for the known risks of the site, Viscusi and Hamilton found that the more times a chemical was mentioned in the popular press, the more stringent was the target (or permissible) risk chosen by the EPA. Thus, instead of cleaning up the most dangerous sites, the EPA is cleaning up the sites that might get the most bad press.

Sadly, the EPA does not seem to care whether the cleanup costs it incurs will actually benefit real people. That is, cleanup decisions generally are unaffected by whether the risks of the site are borne by people who live there today or are hypothetically borne by people who *might someday,* under a worst-case scenario, live near the site. Thus, many cancer cases "prevented" by EPA cleanups are purely hypothetical—benefits likely to materialize only in the minds of EPA employees, who have simply assumed that the Superfund site will one day be a housing subdivision.

The average cost per cancer case averted by the EPA expenditures—$11.7 billion per case—masks enormous variation from site to site. At the most efficiently cleaned-up site, the cost per cancer case averted was but $20,000, surely a good deal by anyone's standards. At the other end of the spectrum, the cost was $961 *billion.* Now, the EPA is not actually spending $961 billion anywhere; indeed, the largest amount spent on any one site was only $134 million. The problem is that the hundreds of millions of dollars poured into the least-efficient cleanups had so little impact that they were essentially a complete waste to society.

According to Viscusi and Hamilton, a key factor leading to the EPA's abysmal decision making is plain old politics. That is, political pressure pushes the EPA into more stringent cleanups, and does so in the worst possible manner. For sites where cleanup is relatively cost-effective, political forces actually have little effect. But at the most inefficient sites, where costs per cancer case averted are in the billions, political factors have their strongest and most wasteful effect.

Although Viscusi and Hamilton focused only on the costs of cancer prevention, the types of problems they discovered appear to be pervasive. Indeed, even Carol Browner, administrator of the EPA under President Clinton, criticized the Superfund program as one that "frequently moves too slowly, cleans up too little, has an unfair liability scheme, and costs too much." How can such a well-intentioned program produce such abysmal results?

There are several reasons. For example, EPA expenditures on Superfund are funded out of special earmarked taxes, rather than from general revenues. Hence the expenditures do not have to pass through the regular congressional appropriation process and are not subject to the budgetary scrutiny that virtually all other federal expenditures must withstand. Moreover, although Superfund was originally sold to Congress—and the nation—on the principle that firms that created the hazards would pay for the cleanup, the industrial taxes that fund EPA's Superfund efforts flagrantly violate this principle. Indeed, chemical and petroleum firms (and certain other large firms in other industries) have to pay the taxes that finance Superfund *regardless* of whether they have ever contaminated an industrial site. Production, not pollution, is taxed to pay for Superfund, meaning that these Superfund taxes create no incentive for firms to operate in a cleaner manner.

In addition to cleanups conducted by the agency itself, the EPA routinely orders firms to clean up other Superfund sites. In these cases, EPA not only does not have to worry about the budgetary consequences of its actions; it also does not have to worry about many other things you might think it would. For example, when EPA orders a firm to clean up a site, it does not have to show that any harm or serious threat of harm has been committed. It only has to show that some harm *might* occur to someone, some time in the future. Similarly, the EPA does not have to show that any law was broken by firms ordered to conduct a cleanup. In fact, most Superfund cleanups are at sites where the environmental damages originally were the result of law-abiding behavior.

It is perhaps even more striking that a firm ordered to perform a cleanup does not even have to be the entity that caused the chemical contamination at the site. It is sufficient that the EPA declare the firm to be a "potentially responsible party"—for example, because the firm once owned the piece of contaminated property. Moreover, in ordering the cleanup, the EPA need not show that the cleanup is either necessary or reasonable, nor that the costs of doing it are reasonable; in fact, the EPA does not have to consider costs at all. As long as the EPA simply follows the procedures it wrote for itself, its decisions have the force of law.

So the problem with the Superfund program is neither bad intentions nor bad people. The problem is a set of institutions, created by Congress, that in turn creates bad incentives. Anyone—private sector, government, or perhaps even a saint—facing similar incentives would likely behave in exactly the manner the EPA does. Thus, if the Superfund program is be improved, the institutions that govern it must be changed. Otherwise, the Superfund follies will continue unabated.

DISCUSSION QUESTIONS

1. If you did not have to bear the costs of your actions, would your behavior be different than it is now? Do you think your behavior would be efficient, that is, would it equate the marginal social costs to the marginal social benefits?

2. If the EPA's Superfund cleanup expenditures were funded out of general revenues, how would competition from other possible uses of those funds likely affect the amount of money going to EPA?

3. If we want to minimize the total cost of preventing a particular number of cancers at Superfund sites, how should we allocate resources across those sites? If we want to maximize the number of cancer cases averted for a given expenditure of resources, how should we allocate resources across Superfund sites? If the EPA fails to meet these criteria for efficient cancer prevention, in what sense can the agency be said to be *causing* cancer?

4. Health and safety are "normal" goods, in the sense that people demand more of them as their income or wealth rises. If we waste resources and this reduces our wealth, what happens to the demand for health and safety—and thus to the amount of health and safety we enjoy? Is it then correct to say that wasteful programs have the effect of killing people?

21

Crime and Punishment

The city of Detroit, Michigan, has twice as many police per capita as Omaha, Nebraska, but the violent crime rate in Detroit is four times as high as in Omaha. Does this mean police are the source of violent crime? If that sounds like an odd question, consider this: Between 1970 and 2000 the number of Americans in prison nearly quadrupled as a share of the population, even as the violent crime rate doubled and the property crime rate rose 30 percent. Does sending people to prison actually encourage them to commit crimes?

Few people would answer either of these questions with a yes, but there is still a widespread concern that crime pays and that there seems to be little that policy makers can do about it. In a nation in which more than 20 percent of all households can expect to be victimized by a serious crime in any given year, it is little wonder that people are asking some tough questions about law enforcement. Do harsher penalties really discourage people from committing crimes? Will longer prison sentences reduce the crime rate? Are more police the answer, or should we try something else? Given that crime costs its victims more than $200 billion every year in America, even as we are spending nearly $100 billion per year in public monies to prevent it, answers to questions such as these are clearly important.

There is one thing we can be sure of at the start: Uniformly heavy punishments for all crimes will lead to a larger number of *major* crimes. Let's look at the reasoning. All decisions are made at the margin. If theft and murder will be punished by the same fate, there is no marginal deterrence to murder. If a theft of $5.00 is met with a punishment of ten years in jail and a theft of $50,000 incurs the same sentence, why not go all the way and steal $50,000? There is no marginal deterrence against committing the bigger theft.

To establish deterrents that are correct at the margin, we must observe empirically how criminals respond to changes in punishments. This leads us to the question of how people decide whether to commit a crime. A theory as to what determines the supply of criminal offenses needs to be established.

Adam Smith, the founder of modern economics, once said

> The affluence of the rich excites the indignation of the poor, who are often both driven by want, and prompted by envy, to invade his possessions. It is only under the shelter of the civil magistrate that the owner of that valuable property, which is acquired by the labour of many years, or perhaps by many successive generations, can sleep a single night in security. He is at all times surrounded by unknown enemies, whom, though he never provokes, he can never appease, and from whose injustice he can be protected only by the powerful arm of the civil magistrate continually held up to chastise it. The acquisition of valuable and extensive property, therefore, necessarily requires the establishment of civil government. Where there is no property, or at least none that exceeds the value of two or three days' labour, civil government is not so necessary.[1]

Thus, Smith concluded, theft will be committed in any society in which one person has substantially more property than another. If Smith is correct, we can surmise that the individuals who engage in theft are seeking income. We can also suppose that, before acting, a criminal might be expected to look at the anticipated costs and returns of criminal activity. These could then be compared with the net returns from legitimate activities. In other words, those engaging in crimes may be thought of as doing so on the basis of a cost/benefit analysis in which the benefits to them outweigh their costs. The benefits of the crime of theft are clear: loot. The costs to the criminal would include, but not be limited to, apprehension by the police, conviction, and jail. The criminal's calculations are thus analogous to those made by an athlete when weighing the cost of possible serious injury against the benefits to be gained from participating in a sport.

---

[1] Adam Smith, *The Wealth of Nations,* 1776.

If we view the supply of offenses in this manner, we can come up with ways in which society can lower the net expected benefit for committing any illegal activity. That is, we can figure out how to reduce crime most effectively. Indeed, economists have applied this sort of reasoning to study empirically the impact of punishment on criminal activity. The two areas on which they have focused are: (1) the impact of increasing the probability that criminals will be detected and apprehended, for example by putting more police on the street; and (2) the role of punishment, for example through imprisonment.

Surprisingly, at least to an economist, the empirical answers to these questions have come back rather mixed. For example, the estimated impact of imprisonment on crime rates appears quite small, indeed often little different from zero. Moreover, a substantial majority of the studies that have attempted to estimate the impact of police on the crime rate have found either no relationship or have found that having more police on the force appears to *increase* the crime rate!

The problem researchers have encountered in estimating the impact of police or prison terms on criminal activity is quite simple in principle but a difficult one to correct: Because people who live in areas with higher crime rates will want to take measures to protect themselves, they are likely to have larger police forces and to punish criminals more severely. Thus even if more police and more severe penalties actually do reduce crime, this true effect may be masked or even seem to be reversed in the data, because high crime areas will tend to have more police and higher prison populations.

Important new research has begun to unravel these influences, however, offering us the clearest picture yet of the likely effects of police and imprisonment on the crime rate. In a series of articles, Steven Levitt of the University of Chicago has looked for factors that strongly influence the number of police in a community or the size of a state's prison population but do not otherwise affect the crime rate.[2] He has found such factors, and in so doing has re-

---

[2] Steven Levitt, "The Effect of Prison Population Size on Crime Rates: Evidence from Prison Overcrowding Litigation," *Quarterly Journal of Economics,* May 1996, pp. 319–351; and "Using Electoral Cycles in Police Hiring to Estimate the Effect of Police on Crime," *American Economic Review,* June 1997, pp. 270–290.

vealed a much clearer picture of the true deterrence effect of law enforcement.

In the case of police, Levitt has found that election cycles tend to have a strong independent effect on the size of police forces, enabling him to identify the impact of police on crime rates. Because crime is such a hot political issue, both mayors and governors have strong incentives (and the ability) to push for more police funding in election years. The result is that even though police forces in major cities tend to remain constant in nonelection years, they grow by about 2 percent in an average election year. Although this may sound small, it is (1) large enough to have a significant impact over several election cycles, and thus (2) large enough to detect clearly in the data.

Levitt finds the strongest deterrent effect of police on violent crime, such as murder, rape, and assault. In fact, he estimates the **elasticity** of violent crime with respect to police to be about –1.0. Thus, for example, a 10 percent increase in a city's police force can be expected to produce about a 10 percent decrease in the violent crime rate in that city. With regard to property crimes, such as burglary, larceny, and auto theft, the impact of having more police is smaller but still significant. In this case, the estimated elasticity is about –0.3, meaning a 10 percent increase in the police force will yield about a 3 percent reduction in property crimes. The implications for a city like Detroit are quite striking. Increasing the police force by 10 percent would mean adding about 440 officers. Levitt's estimates imply that, as a result, the city could expect to suffer about 2100 fewer violent crimes each year and about 2700 fewer property crimes.

To identify the impact of imprisonment on crime rates, Levitt focuses on lawsuits that have been brought against prison systems. These lawsuits, filed in response to prison crowding conditions, have been able to force prison systems to release prisoners. Because the suits do not otherwise affect criminals' decisions, except via their impact on the likelihood of imprisonment, Levitt has been able to isolate the role of imprisonment on deterring crime. He finds once again that the effects are strongest for violent crime: A 10 percent decrease in a state's prison population can be expected to increase the violent crime rate in that state by about 4 percent. In the case of property crime, a 10 percent decrease in prison population will yield about a 3 percent rise in burglaries, larcenies, and auto thefts in the state. One response among states that have been forced to release prisoners has been the construction of new prisons.

In separate research, Levitt has found that juvenile criminals respond to incentives, just as their adult counterparts do. From the mid-1970s to the mid-1990s, juvenile crime soared relative to adult crime, which has led many commentators to worry about a generation of juveniles who are seemingly undaunted by the threat of imprisonment. In fact, it appears soaring juvenile crime was largely the result of changes in the incentives faced by juveniles: Over this same period of time, violent crime imprisonment rates for juveniles fell 80 percent relative to those for adults. Hence, the chances of violent young criminals being jailed dropped to only about half that of violent adult criminals. Moreover, the change in penalties that occurs as youths become subject to adult laws (usually age 18) has a strong effect on their behavior. In states tough on youth but easy on adults, violent crime rates rise 23 percent at age 18, but in states that are easy on juveniles and tough on adults, such crime drops 4 percent at age 18. Incentives, it seems, still matter.

Are the growing expenditures on crime prevention worth it? According to Levitt's results, the answer is yes. Adding another person to the prison population costs about $30,000 per year but can be expected to yield benefits (in terms of crime prevention) of more than $50,000 per year. Although adding an officer to the police force has an expected cost of about $80,000 per year, that officer can be expected to produce crime prevention benefits of almost $200,000. If these numbers are anywhere close to being correct, we can expect further increases in spending on crime prevention in the years to come and perhaps even some noticeable reductions in the crime rate.

DISCUSSION QUESTIONS

1. The analysis just presented seems to make the assumption that criminals act rationally. Does the fact they do not necessarily do so negate the analysis?
2. In many cases, murder is committed among people who know each other. Does this mean that raising the penalty for murder will not affect the number of murders committed?

3. Consider the following prescription for punishments: "Eye for eye, tooth for tooth, hand for hand, foot for foot. . . ." Suppose our laws followed this rule, and further suppose we spent enough money on law enforcement to apprehend everyone who broke the law. What would the crime rate be? (*Hint:* If the penalty for stealing $10 was $10, and if you were certain you would be caught, would there be any expected gain from the theft? Would there be an expected gain from the theft if the penalty were only, say, $1.00, or if the chance of being caught were only 10 percent?)

4. In recent years, the penalty for selling illegal drugs has been increased sharply. How does that affect the incentive to sell drugs? For the people who decide to sell drugs anyway, what do the higher penalties for dealing do to their incentive to commit other crimes (such as murder) while they are engaged in selling drugs?

22

The Graying of America

America is aging. The 78 million baby boomers who pushed the Beatles and the Rolling Stones into stardom are entering middle age. Indeed, the future of America is now on display in Florida, where one person in five is over sixty-five. In thirty years, almost 20 percent of all Americans will be sixty-five or older. Just as the post–World War II baby boom presented both obstacles and opportunities, so too does the graying of America. Let's see why.

Two principal forces are behind America's "senior boom." First, we're living longer. Average life expectancy in 1900 was forty-seven. Today it is seventy-seven and is likely to reach eighty within the next decade. Second, the birth rate is near record low levels. Today's mothers are having *half* the number of children that their mothers had. In short, the old are living longer and the ranks of the young are growing too slowly to offset that fact. Together, these forces are pushing up the proportion of the population over sixty-five; indeed, the population of seniors is growing at twice the rate of the rest of the population. In 1970, the **median age** in the United States—the age that divides the older half of the population from the younger half—was twenty-eight; by 2000 the median age was nearly thirty-six and rising rapidly. Compounding these factors, the average age at retirement has been declining as well, from sixty-five in 1963 to sixty-two currently. The result is more retirees relying on fewer workers to help ensure that their senior years are also golden years.

Why should a person who is, say, college age be concerned with the age of the rest of the population? Well, old people are expensive. In fact, people over sixty-five now consume over one-third of the federal government's budget. Social Security payments to retirees are the biggest item, now running over $300 billion a year. Medicare, which pays hospital and doctors' bills for the elderly, costs over $200 billion a year and is growing rapidly. Moreover, fully a third of the $150-billion-a-year budget for Medicaid, which helps pay medical bills for the poor of all ages, goes to those over the age of sixty-five.

Under current law, the elderly will consume 40 percent of all federal spending within fifteen years: Medicare's share of Gross Domestic Product (GDP) will double, as will the number of very old—those over eighty-five and most in need of care. Within thirty years, probably *one-half* of the federal budget will go to the old. In a nutshell, senior citizens are the beneficiaries of an expensive and rapidly growing share of all federal spending. What are they getting for our dollars?

To begin with, the elderly are already more prosperous than ever. Indeed, the annual discretionary income of those over sixty-five averages 30 percent higher than the average discretionary income of all age groups. Each year, inflation-adjusted Social Security benefits paid new retirees are higher than the first-year benefits paid people who retired the year before. In addition, for the past twenty-five years, cost-of-living adjustments have protected Social Security benefits from inflation. The impact of Social Security is evident even at the lower end of the income scale: The poverty rate for people over sixty-five is much lower than for the population as a whole. Retired people today collect Social Security benefits that are two to five times what they and their employers contributed in payroll taxes, plus interest earned.

Not surprisingly, medical expenses are a major concern for many elderly. Perhaps reflecting that concern, each person under the age of sixty-five in America currently pays an average of roughly $1500 per year in federal taxes to subsidize medical care for the elderly. Indeed, no other country in the world goes to the lengths that America does to preserve life. Some 30 percent of Medicare's budget goes to patients in their last year of life. Coronary bypass operations—costing over $30,000 apiece—are routinely performed on Americans in their sixties and seventies. For those over sixty-five, Medicare picks up the tab. Even heart transplants are now performed on people in their sixties and paid for by Medicare for those over sixty-five. By contrast, the Japanese offer no organ transplants. Britain's National Health Service generally will not provide kidney dialysis for people over fifty-five. Yet Medicare subsidizes dialysis for more than one hundred thousand people, half of them over sixty. The cost: $3 billion a year. Overall, the elderly receive Medicare benefits worth five to twenty times the payroll taxes (plus interest) they paid for this program.

The responsibility for the huge and growing bills for Social Security and Medicare falls squarely on current and future workers, because both programs are financed by taxes on payrolls. Thirty years ago, these programs were adequately financed with a payroll levy of less than 10 percent of the typical worker's earnings. Today, the tax rate exceeds 15 percent of median wages and is expected to grow rapidly.

By the year 2020, early baby boomers, born in the late 1940s and early 1950s, will have retired. Late baby boomers, born in the 1960s, will be nearing retirement. Both groups will leave today's college students, and their children, with a staggering bill to pay. For Social Security and Medicare to stay as they are, the payroll tax rate may have to rise to 25 percent of wages over the next twenty years. And a payroll tax rate of 40 percent is not unlikely by the middle of the twenty-first century.

One way to think of the immense bill facing today's college students, and their successors, is to consider the number of retirees each worker must support. In 1946, the burden of one Social Security recipient was shared by forty-two workers. By 1960, nine workers had to foot the bill for each retiree's Social Security benefits. Today, roughly three workers pick up the tab for each retiree's Social Security, plus his or her Medicare benefits. By 2030, only two workers will be available to pay the Social Security and Medicare benefits due each recipient. Thus a working couple will have to support not only themselves and their family, but also someone outside the family who is receiving Social Security and Medicare benefits.

Paying all the bills presented by the twenty-first century's senior citizens will be made more difficult by another fact: Older workers are leaving the workplace in record numbers. We noted earlier that the average retirement age is down to sixty-two and declining. Only 30 percent of the people age fifty-five and over hold jobs today, compared with 45 percent in 1930. Thus even as the elderly are making increasing demands on the federal budget, fewer of them are staying around to help foot the bill.

Part of the exodus of the old from the workplace is due simply to their prosperity. Older people have higher disposable incomes than any other age group in the population and are using it to consume more leisure. Importantly, however, the changing work habits of older individuals have been prompted—perhaps inadvertently—by American businesses. Career advancement often slows after age forty—over 60 percent of American corporations offer early retirement plans, whereas only about 5 percent offer inducements to delay retirement. Looking ahead to career dead-ends and hefty retirement checks, increasing numbers of older workers are opting for the golf course instead of the morning commute.

Recently, however, the private sector has begun to realize that the graying of America requires that we rethink the role of senior citizens in the workforce. Some firms are doing more than just thinking. For example, a major chain of home centers in California has begun vigorously recruiting senior citizens as salesclerks. The result has been a sharp increase in customer satisfaction: The older workers know the merchandise better and have more experience in dealing with people. Moreover, turnover and absenteeism have plummeted. People with gray hair, it seems, are immune to "surfer's throat," a malady that strikes younger Californians before sunny weekends.

Other firms have introduced retirement transition programs. Instead of early retirement at age fifty-five or sixty, for example, older workers are encouraged to simply cut back on their workweek while staying on the job. Often, it is possible for workers to get the best of both worlds, collecting a retirement check even while working part-time at the same firm. Another strategy recognizes the importance of rewarding superior performance among older workers. At some firms, for example, senior technical managers are relieved of the drudgery of mundane management tasks and allowed to spend more time focusing on the technical side of their specialties. To sweeten the pot, a pay hike is often included in the package.

Apparently, programs such as these are beginning to pay off. In one recent survey, more than 70 percent of the four hundred businesses queried gave their older workers top marks for job performance; over 80 percent of the seniors received ratings of excellent or very good for their commitment to quality. Moreover, many firms are finding that the retention of older workers cuts training and pension costs sharply and, because older workers are less likely to have school-age children, even reduces health insurance outlays.

Congress and the president thus far seem unwilling to face the pitfalls and promises of an aging America. Although the age of retirement for Social Security purposes is legislatively mandated to rise to sixty-seven from sixty-five, the politicians in Washington, D.C., appear unable to do anything else but appoint commissions to "study" the problems we face—problems that rapidly worsen as the studies pile up. And all the while, there are some solutions out there. Chile, for example, faced a national pension system with even more severe problems than our Social Security system. Its response was to transform the system into one that is rapidly (and automatically, as time passes) converting itself into a completely private pension system. The result has been security for existing retirees, higher potential benefits for future retirees, and lower taxes for all workers. Americans could do exactly what the Chileans have done—if we chose to do so.

Many experts believe that significant changes in America's immigration laws could offer the best hope of dealing with the tax burdens and workforce shrinkage of the future. About a million immigrants come to America each year, the largest number in our nation's history. Yet more than 90 percent of new immigrants are admitted based on a selection system unchanged since 1952, under which the right of immigration is tied to family preference. As a result, most people are admitted to the United States because they happen to be the spouses, children, or siblings of earlier immigrants, rather than because they have skills or training highly valued in the American workplace. Both Canada and Australia have modified their immigration laws to expand opportunities for those immigrants who possess skills in short supply, with results that are generally regarded quite favorably in both nations. Unless Congress manages to overhaul America's immigration preference system, new immigrants are unlikely to relieve much of the pressure building due to our aging population.

In the meantime, if Social Security and Medicare are kept on their current paths, and older workers continue to be taxed out of the workforce, the future burden on those who are today's college students is likely to be unbearable. If we are to avoid the social tension and enormous costs of such an outcome, the willingness and ability of older individuals to retain more of their self-sufficiency must be recognized. To do otherwise is to invite a future in which the golden years are but memories of the past.

DISCUSSION QUESTIONS

1. How do the payroll taxes levied on the earnings of workers affect their decisions about how much leisure they consume?

2. When the government taxes younger people so as to pay benefits to older people, how does this affect the amount of assistance that younger people might voluntarily choose to offer older people?

3. When the government taxes younger people so as to pay benefits to older people, how does this affect the size of the bequests that older people are likely to leave to their children or grandchildren when they die?

4. In general, people who are more productive earn higher incomes and thus pay higher taxes. How would a change in the immigration law that favored more highly educated and skilled individuals affect the future tax burden of today's American college students? Would the admission of better-educated immigrants tend to raise or lower the wages of American college graduates? On balance, would an overhaul of the immigration system benefit or harm today's college students?

Part Six

Property Rights and the Environment

INTRODUCTION

We saw in Part Four that monopoly produces outcomes that differ significantly from the competitive outcome and so yields gains from trade that fall short of the competitive ideal. In Part Six we see that when externalities are present—that is, when there are discrepancies between the private costs of action and the social costs of action—the competitive outcome differs from the competitive ideal. Typically, the problem in the case of externalities is said to be *market failure,* but the diagnosis might just as well be termed *government failure.* For markets to work efficiently, property rights to scarce goods must be clearly defined, cheaply enforceable, and fully transferable, and it is generally the government that is believed to have a comparative advantage in ensuring that these conditions are satisfied. If the government fails to define, enforce, or make transferable property rights, the market will generally fail to produce socially efficient outcomes, and it becomes a moot point as to who is at fault. The real point is this: What might be done to improve things?

As population and per capita income both rise, consumption rises faster than either, for it responds to the combined impetus of both. With consumption comes the residue of consumption, also known as plain old garbage. Many of us have heard of landfills being closed because of fears of groundwater contamination, or of homeless garbage scows wandering the high seas in search of a place to off-load; all of us have been bombarded with public service messages to recycle everything from aluminum cans to old newspapers. The United States, it seems, is becoming the garbage capital of the world. This is no doubt true, but it is also true that the United States is the professional football capital of the world—and yet pro football teams seem to have no problem finding cities across the country willing to welcome them with open arms. What is different about garbage? You probably are inclined to answer that football is enjoyable and garbage is not. True enough, but this is not why garbage sometimes piles up faster than anyone seems willing to dispose of it. Garbage becomes a problem only if it is not priced properly; that is, if the consumers and businesses that produce it are not charged enough for its removal, and the landfills where it is deposited are not paid enough for its disposal. The message of Chapter 23, "The Trashman Cometh," is that garbage really is not different from the things we consume in the course of producing it. As long as the trashman is paid, he will cometh, and as long as we have to pay for his services, his burden will be bearable. We will still have garbage, but we will not have a garbage problem.

We noted earlier that the property rights to a scarce good or resource must be clearly defined, fully enforced, and readily transferable if that resource is to be used efficiently—that is, in the manner that yields the greatest net benefits. This is true whether the resource in question is space in a landfill, water in a stream, or, as we see in Chapter 24, "Bye, Bye, Bison," members of an animal species. If these conditions are satisfied, the resource will be used in the manner that benefits both its owner and society the most. If these conditions are not satisfied—as they were not for American bison on the hoof or passenger pigeons on the wing—the resource generally will not be used in the most efficient manner. And in the case of animal species that are competing with human beings, this sometimes means extinction. What should be done when a species becomes endangered? If our desire is to produce the greatest net benefit to humanity, the answer in general is not to protect the species at *any* possible cost, for this would be equivalent to assigning an infinite value to the species. Instead, the proper course of action is to devise rules that induce people to act as though the members of the species were private property. If such rules can be developed, we shall not have to worry about spotted owls or

African elephants becoming extinct any more than we currently worry about parakeets or cocker spaniels becoming extinct.

In Chapter 25, "Smog Merchants," property rights are again the focus of the discussion as we look at air pollution. We ordinarily think of the air around us as being something that we all own. The practical consequence of this is that we act as though the air is owned by none of us—for no one can exclude anyone else from using our air. As a result, we overuse the air in the sense that air pollution becomes a problem. This chapter shows that it is possible to define and enforce property rights to air, which the owners can then use as they see fit—which includes selling the rights to others. Once this is done, the users of clean air have the incentive to use it just as efficiently as they do all of the other resources (such as land, labor, and capital) utilized in the production process.

Air—or more generally, the atmosphere as a whole—reappears as the topic of Chapter 26, "Greenhouse Economics." There is a growing body of evidence that human action is responsible for rising concentrations of so-called greenhouse gases in the earth's atmosphere, and that left unchecked this growth may produce costly increases in the average temperature of our planet. Given the nature of the problem—a **negative externality**—private action taken on the individual level will not yield the optimal outcome for society. Thus the potential gains from government action, in the form of environmental regulations or taxation, are substantial. The key word here is potential, for government action, no matter how well-intentioned, does not automatically yield benefits that exceed the costs. As we seek solutions to the potential problems associated with greenhouse gases, we must be sure that the consequences of premature action are not worse than those of first examining the problem further. If we forget this message, greenhouse economics may turn into bad economics—and worse policy.

One important class of property rights issues arises for commodities called **public goods**. These are goods that have two characteristics: Consumption by one person does not diminish the amount available for others to consume, and it is extremely costly to prevent nonpaying individuals from consuming the goods. These characteristics make it difficult for the private sector to provide the appropriate amount of such goods, meaning that the government sometimes must step in and do the job. In Chapter 27, "The Economics of

Weather Forecasting," we take a trip back in time to examine the costs and benefits associated with the founding of what was to become the U.S. Weather Service. Here the public good in question was information on weather storm warnings on the Great Lakes. Although it will never be known whether the private sector could have done the job better, we find that the government's earliest attempts at weather forecasting were good enough to yield positive net gains to society.

Although forest areas in the United States and much of Europe are growing, this is in sharp contrast to much of the rest of the world, where forests appear to be shrinking. As we see in Chapter 28, "Property Rights and Forests," this contrast can be explained quite simply. When property rights to forests are secure, as they are in the United States and much of Europe, private owners husband them in an efficient manner. But where those property rights are insecure, harvesting rates are much higher and replanting rates much lower, yielding sharp downward pressure on forest stocks. It also turns out that property rights are important for government management of forests, just as they are for private sector management: As we see in this chapter, when the benefits of government-managed forests accrue to clearly defined individuals or groups, those governments do a much more efficient—and environmentally friendly—job of managing those forests. Incentives, it seem, matter everywhere.

23

The Trashman Cometh

Is garbage really different? To answer this question, let us consider a simple hypothetical situation. Suppose a city agreed to provide its residents with all of the food they wished to consume, prepared in the manner they specified, and delivered to their homes for a flat, monthly fee that was independent of what or how much they ate. What are the likely consequences of this city food delivery service? Most likely, people in the city would begin to eat more, because the size of their food bill would be independent of the amount they ate. They would also be more likely to consume lobster and filet mignon rather than fish sticks and hamburger because, once again, the cost to them would be independent of their menu selections. Soon the city's food budget would be astronomical, and either the monthly fee or taxes would have to be increased. People from other communities might even begin moving (or at least making extended visits) to the city, just to partake of this wonderful service. Within short order the city would face a food crisis as it sought to cope with providing a rapidly growing amount of food from a city budget that could no longer handle the financial burden.

If this story sounds silly to you, just change "food delivery" to "garbage pickup"; what we have just described is the way most cities in the country historically have operated their municipal garbage collection services. The result during the late 1980s and early 1990s was the appearance of a garbage crisis—with overflowing landfills, homeless garbage scows, and drinking-water wells polluted with the runoff from trash heaps. This seeming crisis—to the extent it existed—was fundamentally no different from the food crisis described above. The problem was not that (1) almost nobody wants garbage, nor that (2) garbage has adverse environmental effects, nor even that (3) we had too much garbage. The problem lay in that (1) we ordinarily do not put prices on garbage in the way we put prices on the goods that generate the garbage, and (2) a strange assortment of bedfellows used a few smelly facts to make things seem worse than they were.

First things first. America is producing garbage at a record rate: In 1999 we generated about 210 million tons of household and commercial solid waste that either had to be burned or buried. (That works out to almost 1500 pounds per person.) About 40 percent of this was paper, whereas yard waste (such as grass trimmings) accounted for another 15 percent. Plastics amounted to about 20 percent of the volume of material that had to be disposed of, but because plastic is relatively light, it comprised only about 9 percent of the weight. Had there been no recycling, probably we would have had to dispose of another 40 to 50 million tons of assorted trash.

Landfills are the final resting place for most of our garbage, although incineration is also widely used in some areas, particularly in the Northeast, where land values are high. Both methods began falling out of favor with people who lived near these facilities (or might eventually), as NIMBY (not-in-my-backyard) attitudes spread across the land. Federal, state, and local regulations also made it increasingly difficult to establish new waste disposal facilities, or even to keep old ones operating. The cost to open a modern 100-acre landfill rose to an estimated $70 million or more, and the permit process needed to open a new disposal facility soared to seven years in some states. Meanwhile, environmental concerns forced the closure of many landfills throughout the country and prevented others from ever beginning operations. By 1992, all but five states were exporting at least some of their garbage to other states. Today, most of the garbage from some densely populated states in the Northeast ends up in other people's backyards: New Jersey ships garbage to ten other states, while New York keeps landfill operators busy in thirteen different states. Across the country, Americans have begun to wonder where all of the garbage is going to go.

Although the failure of America's cities to price garbage appropriately led to an inefficient amount of the stuff, much of the appearance of a garbage crisis has been misleading. Rubbish first hit the headlines in 1987 when a garbage barge named *Mobro*, headed south with New York City trash, couldn't find a home for its load. As it turns out, the barge operator hadn't nailed down a satisfactory disposal contract before he sailed; when he tried to conduct negotiations over the radio while under way, operators of likely landfills (mistakenly) suspected he might be carrying toxic waste rather than routine trash. When adverse publicity forced the barge back to New York with its load, many people thought it was a lack of landfill space, rather than poor planning by the barge operator, that was the cause. This notion was reinforced by an odd combination of environmental groups, waste management firms, and the Environmental Protection Agency (EPA).

The Environmental Defense Fund wanted to start a major campaign to push recycling, and the *Mobro* gave things the necessary push. As one official for the organization noted, "An advertising firm couldn't have designed a better vehicle than a garbage barge." Meanwhile, a number of farsighted waste management companies had begun loading up on landfill space, taking advantage of new technologies that increased the efficient minimum size of a disposal facility. Looking to get firm contracts for filling this space, the trade group for the disposal industry started pushing the notion that America was running out of dump space. State and local officials who relied on the group's data quickly bought into the new landfills, paying premium prices to do so. The EPA, meanwhile, was studying the garbage problem but without accounting for the fact that its own regulations were causing the efficient scale of landfills to double and even quadruple in size. Thus the EPA merely counted landfills around the country and reported that they were shrinking in number. This was true enough, but what the EPA failed to report was that because landfills were getting bigger much faster than they were closing down, total disposal capacity was *growing* rapidly, not shrinking.

For a while, it seemed that recycling was going to take care of what appeared to be a growing trash problem. In 1987, for example, old newspapers were selling for as much as $60 per ton, and many municipalities felt that the answer to their financial woes and garbage troubles was at hand. Yet as more communities began putting mandatory recycling laws into effect, the prices of recycled trash began to plummet. Over the next five years, 3500 communities in more than half the states had some form of mandatory curbside recycling; the resulting increase in the supply of used newsprint meant that communities soon were having to pay to have the stuff carted away—a situation that continues today. For glass and plastics, the story is so far much the same: The market value of the used materials is below the cost of collecting and sorting it. About a dozen states have acted to increase the demand for old newsprint by requiring locally published newspapers to utilize a minimum content of recycled newsprint. Even so, many experts believe that no more than 60 to 70 percent of all newsprint can be recycled, and we are already recycling 52 percent of it, up from 33 percent in 1988.

Just as significantly, recycling raises significant issues that were often ignored during the early rush to embrace the concept. For example, the production of a hundred tons of de-inked fiber from old newsprint produces about forty tons of sludge that must be disposed of somehow. Although the total volume of material is reduced, the concentrated form of what is left can make it more costly to dispose of properly. Similarly, recycling paper is unlikely to save trees, for most virgin newsprint is made from trees planted expressly for that purpose and harvested as a crop: If recycling increases, many of these trees simply will not be planted. In a study done for Resources for the Future, A. Clark Wiseman concluded, "The likely effect of [newsprint recycling] appears to be smaller, rather than larger, forest inventory." Moreover, most virgin newsprint is made in Canada, using clean hydroelectric power. Makers of newsprint in the United States (the primary customers for the recycled stuff) often use higher-polluting energy such as coal. Thus one potential side effect of recycling is the switch from hydroelectric power to fossil fuels.

Some have argued that we should simply ban certain products. For example, styrofoam cups have gotten a bad name because they take up more space in landfills than do paper hot-drink cups, and because styrofoam remains in the landfill forever. Yet according to a widely cited study by Martin B. Hockman of the University of Victoria, the manufacture of a paper cup consumes 36 times as much electricity and generates 580 times as much wastewater as does the manufacture of a styrofoam cup. Moreover, as paper degrades underground, it releases methane, a greenhouse gas that contributes to warming the atmosphere. In a similar vein, consider disposable diapers, which have been trashed by their opponents because a week's worth generates 22.2 pounds of post-use waste, whereas a week's worth of reusable diapers generates only 0.24 pound. Because disposable diapers already amount to 2 percent of the nation's solid waste, the edge clearly seems to go to reusable cloth diapers. Yet the use of reusable rather than disposable diapers consumes more than three times as many Btus (British thermal units) of energy and generates ten times as much water pollution. It would seem that the trade-offs that are present when we talk about "goods" are just as prevalent when we discuss "bads" such as garbage.

It also appears that more government regulation of the garbage business is likely to make things worse rather than better, as may be illustrated by the tale of two states: New Jersey and Pennsylvania. A number of years ago, to stop what was described as price-gouging by organized crime, New Jersey decided to regulate waste hauling and disposal as a public utility. Once the politicians got involved in the trash business, however, politics very nearly destroyed the business of trash. According to Paul Kleindorfer of the University of Pennsylvania, political opposition to passing garbage disposal costs along to consumers effectively ended investment in landfills. In 1972 there were 331 landfills operating in New Jersey; by 1988 the number had fallen to 13, because the state-regulated fees payable to landfill operators simply didn't cover the rising costs of operation. Half of New Jersey's municipal solid waste is now exported to neighboring Pennsylvania.

Pennsylvania's situation provides a sharp contrast. The state does not regulate the deals that communities make with landfill and incinerator operators; the market takes care of matters instead. For example, despite the state's hands-off policy, tipping fees (the charges for disposing of garbage in landfills) are below the national average in Pennsylvania, effectively limited by competition between disposal facilities. The market seems to be providing the right incentives; in one recent year, there were thirty-one pending applications to open landfills in Pennsylvania, but only two in New Jersey, despite the fact that New Jersey residents are paying the highest disposal rates in the country to ship garbage as far away as Michigan, Illinois, Missouri, and Alabama.

Ultimately, there are two issues that must be solved when it comes to trash. First, what do we do with it once we have it? Second, how do we reduce the amount of it that we have? As hinted at by the Pennsylvania story and illustrated further by developments elsewhere in the country, the market mechanism can answer both questions. The fact of the matter is that in many areas of the country, population densities are high and land is expensive. Hence a large amount of trash is produced, and it is expensive to dispose of locally. In contrast, there are some areas of the country where there are relatively few people around to produce garbage, where land for disposal facilities is cheap, and where wide-open spaces minimize the potential air pollution hazards associated with incinerators. The sensible thing to do, it would seem, is to have the states that produce most of the trash ship it to states where it can be most efficiently disposed of—for a price, of course. This is already being done to an extent, but residents of potential recipient states are (not surprisingly) concerned, lest they end up being the garbage capitals of the nation. Yet Wisconsin, which imports garbage from as far away as New Jersey, is demonstrating that it is possible to get rid of the trash without trashing the neighborhood. Landfill operators in Wisconsin are now required to send water table monitoring reports to neighbors and to maintain the landfills for forty years after closure. Operators also have guaranteed the value of neighboring homes to gain the permission of nearby residents and in some cases have purchased homes to quiet neighbors' objections. These features all add to the cost of operating landfills, but as long as prospective customers are willing to pay the price and neighboring residents are satisfied with their protections—and so far these conditions appear to be satisfied—then it would seem tough to argue with the outcome.

Some might still argue that it does not seem right for one community to be able to dump its trash elsewhere. Yet the flip side is this: Is it right to *prevent* communities from accepting the trash, if that is what they want? Consider Gilliam County, Oregon (pop. 1,950), which wanted Seattle's garbage so badly it fought Oregon state legislators' attempts to tax out-of-state trash coming into Oregon. Seattle's decision to use the Gilliam County landfill generated $1 million per year for the little community—some 25 percent of its annual budget and enough to finance the operations of the county's largest school.

Faced with the prospect of paying to dispose of its garbage, Seattle quickly had to confront the problem of reducing the amount of trash its residents were generating. Its solution was to charge householders according to the amount they put out. Seattle thus began charging $16.10 per month for each can picked up weekly. Yard waste that has been separated for composting costs $4.25 per month, and paper, glass, and metal separated for recycling are hauled away at no charge. In the first year that per-can charges were imposed, the total tonnage that had to be buried fell by 22 percent. Voluntary recycling rose from 24 percent of waste to 36 percent—a rate almost triple the national average at the time. The "Seattle Stomp" (used to fit more trash into a can) became a regular source of exercise, and the city had trouble exporting enough garbage to fulfill its contract with Gilliam County.

The Seattle experience is paralleled by a similar program in Charlottesville, VA. A few years ago, this university town of 40,000 began charging $0.80 per 32-gallon bag or can of residential garbage collected at the curb. The results of the city's new policy suggest that people respond to garbage prices just as they do to all other prices: When an activity becomes more expensive, people engage in less of it. In fact, after controlling for other factors, the introduction of this unit-pricing plan induced people to reduce the volume of garbage presented for collection by 37 percent.

Where did all of the garbage go? Well, some of it didn't go anywhere, because many residents began practicing their own version of the Seattle Stomp, compacting garbage into fewer bags. Even so, the total weight of Charlottesville's garbage dropped by 14 percent in response to unit pricing. Not all of this represented a reduction in garbage production, because some residents resorted to "midnight dumping"—tossing their trash into commercial dumpsters or their neighbors' cans during late-night forays. This sort of behavior is much like the rise in gasoline thefts that occurred in the 1970s when gas prices jumped to the equivalent of $3 to $4 per gallon. But just as locking gas caps ended most gas thefts, there may be a simple way to prevent most midnight dumping. Economists who have studied the Charlottesville program in detail suggest that property taxes or monthly fees could be used to cover the cost of one bag per household each week, with a price per bag applied only to additional bags. According to these estimates, a one-bag allowance would stop all midnight dumping by most one-person households and stop almost half the dumping by a hypothetical three-person household. Moreover, such a scheme would retain most of the environmental benefits of the garbage pricing program.

The message slowly beginning to emerge across the country then, is that garbage really is not different from the things we consume in the course of producing it. As long as the trashman is paid, he will cometh, and as long as we must pay for his services, his burden will be bearable.

DISCUSSION QUESTIONS

1. How do deposits on bottles and cans affect the incentives of individuals to recycle these products?

2. Why do many communities mandate recycling? Is it possible to induce people to recycle more without requiring that all residents recycle?

3. How do hefty per-can garbage pickup fees influence the decisions people make about what goods they will consume?

4. A community planning on charging a fee for trash pickup might structure the fee in any of several ways. It might, for example, charge (1) a fixed amount per can; (2) an amount per pound of garbage; or (3) a flat fee per month, without regard to amount of garbage. How would each of these affect the amount and type of garbage produced? Which system would lead to an increase in the use of trash compactors? Which would lead to the most garbage?

24

Bye, Bye, Bison

The destruction of animal species by humans is nothing new. For example, the arrival of human beings in North America about 12,000 years ago is tied to the extinction of most of the megafauna (very large animals) which then existed. The famous LaBrea Tarpits of southern California yielded the remains of twenty-four mammals and twenty-two birds that no longer exist. Among these are the saber-toothed tiger, the giant llama, the twenty-foot ground sloth, and a bison that stood seven feet at the hump and had six-foot-wide horns.

Although many experts believe that human hunting was directly responsible for the destruction of these species, and that a combination of hunting and habitat destruction by humans has led to the extinction of many other species, the link is not always as clear as it might seem at first glance. For example, it is estimated that only about 0.02 percent (1 in 5000) of all species that have ever existed are currently extant. Most of these (including the dinosaurs) disappeared long before humans ever made an appearance. The simple fact is that all species compete for the limited resources available, and most species have been out-competed, with or without the help of *Homo sapiens.* Just as important is that basic economic principles can help explain why various species are more or less prone to meet their demise at the hands of humans, and what humans might do if they want to delay the extinction of any particular species.[1]

Let's begin with the passenger pigeon, which provides the most famous example of the role of human beings in the extinction of a

---

[1] We say "delay" rather than "prevent" extinction because there is no evidence to date that any species—*Homo sapiens* included—has any claim on immortality.

species. At one time these birds were the most numerous species of birds in North America and perhaps in the world. They nested and migrated together in huge flocks and probably numbered in the billions. When flocks passed overhead, the sky would be dark with pigeons for days at a time. The famous naturalist John James Audubon measured one roost at forty miles long and three miles wide, with birds stacked from treetop down to nearly ground level. Although the Native Americans had long hunted these birds, the demise of the passenger pigeon is usually tied to the arrival of the white man, which increased the demand for pigeons as a source of food and sport. The birds were shot and netted in vast numbers; by the end of the nineteenth century, an animal species that had been looked on as almost indestructible because of its enormous numbers had almost completely disappeared. The last known passenger pigeon died in the Cincinnati Zoo in 1914.

The American bison only narrowly escaped the same fate. The vast herds that roamed the plains were an easy target for hunters; with the advent of the railroad and the need to feed railroad crews as the transcontinental railroads were built, hunters such as Buffalo Bill Cody killed bison by the thousands. As the demand for the fur of the bison increased, it became the target for more hunting. Like the passenger pigeon, the bison had appeared to be indestructible because of its huge numbers, but the species was soon on the way to becoming extinct. Despite the outcries of the Native Americans who found their major food source being decimated, it was not until late in the nineteenth century that any efforts were made to protect the bison.[2]

These two episodes, particularly that of the bison, are generally viewed as classic examples of humankind's inhumanity to our fellow species, as well as to our fellow humans, for many Native American tribes were ultimately devastated by the near demise of the bison. A closer look reveals more than simply wasteful slaughter; it discloses exactly why events progressed as they did and how we can learn from them to improve modern efforts to protect species threatened by human neighbors.

---

[2] For the bison's cousin, the eastern buffalo—which stood seven feet tall at the shoulder, was twelve feet long, and weighed more than a ton—the efforts came too late. The last known members of the species, a cow and her calf, were killed in 1825 in the Allegheny Mountains.

Native Americans had hunted the bison for many years before the arrival of white men and are generally portrayed as both carefully husbanding their prey and generously sharing the meat among tribal members. Yet the braves who rode their horses into the thundering herds marked their arrows so it was clear who had killed the bison. The marked arrows gave the shooter rights to the best parts of the animal. Tribal members who specialized in butchering the kill also received a share as payment for processing the meat. Indeed, the Native American hunting parties were organized remarkably like the parties of the white men who followed: *Once they were killed,* the ownership of the bison was clearly defined, fully enforced, and readily transferable. Moreover, the rewards were distributed in accord with the contribution that each had made to the overall success of the hunt.

Matters were different when it came to the ownership rights to living bison herds. Native Americans, like the whites who came later, had no economically practical way to fence in the herds. The bison could (and did) migrate freely from one tribe's territory into the territory of other tribes. If the members of one tribe economized on their kill, their conservation efforts would chiefly provide more meat for another tribe, who might well be their mortal enemies. This fact induced Native Americans to exploit the bison, so that the herds disappeared from some traditional territories on the Great Plains by 1840—before Buffalo Bill was even born.

Two factors made the efforts of the white man—the railroad hunters—more destructive, hastening the disappearance of the bison herds. First, the white population (and thus the demand for the meat and hides) was much larger than the Native American population. Second, white men used firearms on the bison—a technological revolution that increased the killing capacity of a given hunter by a factor of 20 or more, compared to the bow and arrow. Nevertheless, the fundamental problem was the same for the white man and Native American alike: The property rights to live bison could not be cheaply established and enforced. To own a bison one had to kill it, and so too many bison were killed.

The property rights to a scarce good or resource must be clearly defined, fully enforced, and readily transferable if that resource is to be used efficiently—that is, in the manner that yields the greatest net benefits. This is true whether the resource in question is the

American bison, the water in a stream, or a pepperoni pizza. If these conditions are satisfied, the resource will be used in the manner that best benefits both its owner and society.[3] If they are not satisfied—as they were not for bison on the hoof or passenger pigeons on the wing—the resource generally will not be used in the most efficient manner. In the case of animal species that are competing with human beings, this sometimes means extinction.

In modern times, the government has attempted to limit hunting and fishing seasons and the number of animals that may be taken by imposing state and federal regulations. The results have been at least partially successful. It is likely, for example, that there are more deer in North America today than there were at the time of the colonists—a fact that is not entirely good news for people whose gardens are sometimes the target of hungry herds. In effect, a rationing system (other than prices) is being used in an attempt to induce hunters and fishermen to act as though the rights to migratory animals were clearly defined, fully enforced, and readily transferable. Yet the threatened extinction of many species of whales illustrates that the problem is far from resolved.

The pattern of harvesting whales has been the subject of international discussion ever since World War II, for migratory whales are like nineteenth-century bison: To own them, one must kill them. It was readily apparent to all concerned that without some form of restraint, many species of whales were in danger of extinction. The result was the founding of the International Whaling Commission (IWC) in 1948, which attempted to regulate international whaling. But the IWC was virtually doomed from the start, for its members had the right to veto any regulation they considered too restrictive, and the commission had no enforcement powers in the event a member nation chose to disregard the rules. Moreover, some whaling nations (such as Chile and Peru) refused to join the IWC, so commission quotas had little effect on them. Some IWC members have used nonmember flagships to circumvent agreed-upon quotas,

[3] See Ronald Coase, "The Problem of Social Cost," *Journal of Law & Economics,* October 1960, pp. 1–44. This does not mean that all species will be permanently protected from extinction, for reasons that are suggested in Chapter 3, "Flying the Friendly Skies?" It does mean that extinction will be permitted to occur only if the benefits of doing so exceed the costs.

while others have claimed that they were killing the whales solely for exempt "research" purposes.

The story of the decimation of a species is well told in the events surrounding blue whales, which are believed to migrate thousands of miles each year. This animal, which sometimes weighs almost 100 tons, is difficult to kill even with the most modern equipment; nevertheless, intensive hunting gradually reduced the stock from somewhere between 300,000 and 1 million to, at present, somewhere between 600 and 3000. In the 1930–1931 winter season, almost 30,000 blue whales were taken, a number far in excess of the species' ability to replenish through reproduction. Continued intense harvesting brought the catch down to fewer than 10,000 by 1945–1946, and in the late 1950s the yearly harvest was down to around 1500 per year. By 1964–1965, whalers managed to find and kill only 20 blue whales. Despite a 1965 ban by the IWC, the hunting of blues continued by nonmembers such as Brazil, Chile, and Peru.

Humpback whales have suffered a similar fate. From an original population estimated at 300,000, there remain fewer than 5000 today. Like the blues, humpbacks are now under a hunting ban, but the lack of monitoring and enforcement capacity on the part of the IWC makes it likely that some harvesting is still taking place. IWC conservation attempts designed to protect finbacks, minke whales, and sperm whales have also been circumvented, most notably by the Russians and Japanese, who have simply announced their own unilateral quotas.

Whales are not the only seagoing creatures to suffer from an absence of clearly defined, cheaply enforceable, and transferable property rights. Codfish off the New England and eastern Canadian coasts were once so abundant, it was said, that a person could walk across the sea on their backs. The fish grew into six-foot-long, 200-pound giants, and generations of families from coastal communities knew they could count on the fish for a prosperous livelihood. The problem was that, to establish rights to that bounty, the fish first had to be hauled from the sea. The result was overfishing, which led to declining yields and shrinking fish. Over the last thirty years alone, the catch has dropped more than 75 percent, and the typical fish caught these days weighs but twenty pounds. As a result, the Canadians have virtually closed down their cod fishery, and the American fleet is but a ghost of its former self.

The cod is not alone in its demise. In the northeastern Atlantic, haddock, mackerel, and herring are all in serious trouble. Along the West Coast of the United States, lingcod, rockfish, and bocaccio are in trouble as well. Worldwide, 30 percent of fish stocks, including orange roughy, shark, swordfish, and tuna, are declining due to overfishing, and another 40 percent or more of the commercial stocks are on the verge of trouble.

A number of nations have taken legislative action in the hope of stemming the decline. Beginning in 1996, for example, the U.S. National Maritime Fisheries Service was required to begin working with eight regional fishing councils around the country to come up with plans to stem the demise of traditional fish stocks. Yet not all the councils are actually following the plans they have laid out, so the overfishing continues. A more promising approach may be seen in Britain, where under the terms of European Union rules, the catch of all major fish stocks are limited by quotas, which specify the amount of fish that legally may be taken. The British innovation has been to make those quotas transferable—that is, the rights to catch specific numbers of fish can be purchased and sold just like any other goods. The quotas assign rights to fish, and their transferability ensures that the lowest-cost, most sensible means of taking those fish will be used. With quotas set at levels consistent with the long-term survival of the fish, and the elimination of the pressure to "catch it or lose it," fish stocks in the affected areas seemed to have begun a turnaround.

Even where government regulations attempt to protect animals, poaching has been widespread because it is a lucrative source of income. During the 1980s, the population of African elephants was cut sharply, with most of the decimation coming at the hands of poachers. In African nations where average annual income is only a few hundred dollars per person, it is little wonder that the elephant—whose tusks brought up to $6000 per pair—was a prize target of poachers. An international ban on trade in ivory from 1989 to 1997 helped drive the price of tusks down, offering the African elephant some respite. Yet as we saw in Chapter 5, "Sex, Booze, and Drugs," when buyer and seller are willing participants in a transaction, government bans on exchange are unlikely to be an effective long-term solution.

Nevertheless, a comparison of the experiences of various African nations suggests how a different type of government action can play a pivotal role in determining the long-term survival chances of the African elephant and other endangered species. In South Africa, where the government has allowed controlled culls (at hefty fees) and plowed the proceeds into protecting herds from poachers, the elephant population actually grew during the late 1980s, even before the ban on the ivory trade began, and continues growing rapidly today. The nation of Burundi, which exported more than 20,000 elephant tusks each year during the 1980s, provides a sharp contrast. Internationally recognized elephant counts reveal that only one (yes, one) elephant actually lived in Burundi. Nevertheless, year after year, the government of that nation certified that all of the country's tusk exports were harvested within Burundi's borders rather than poached elsewhere. One can only wonder how that solitary, prolific pachyderm did it—and what share of the profits was going to government officials.

By taking the approach of the South African government one step further, the African nation of Zimbabwe offers some hope that the creation and enforcement of property rights in live elephants and other wildlife may ultimately protect the species from extinction. The government of Zimbabwe has established a program known as CAMPFIRE (Communal Area Programme for Indigenous Resources), which is based on the principle that the benefits from wildlife must go to those who bear the costs of having to coexist with wild animals. In effect, local inhabitants are encouraged to profit from wildlife resources. During the program's first year of existence, permits were sold to hunt fourteen elephants, eighty-two cape buffalo, and twety-six lions and leopards, generating more than $120,000 in revenues. The program now generates revenues of several million dollars per year, 60 percent of which goes to local villages and 20 percent of which goes to government conservation projects, including antipoaching patrols. In addition, meat from sport hunting and herd culls is distributed to the natives, who are also compensated for wildlife-caused damage to crops and livestock. There is now also a growing photographic safari industry in Zimbabwe. A report by the World Wildlife Fund estimates that the CAMPFIRE program has increased household incomes by 15 to 25 percent.

The effectiveness of the CAMPFIRE program has been hampered to some extent by the resistance to change by local bureaucracies. There also has been corruption that has diverted some funds from the local inhabitants who must bear the costs of living with animals that destroy crops and people. Nevertheless, the overall results are striking. Poaching has all but disappeared in these regions, and land has been taken out of agricultural production to provide more wildlife habitat. The local peoples have begun to view wild animals as valuable assets, rather than solely as dangerous nuisances. As for the elephants, well, their numbers are growing at five percent a year in Zimbabwe, as local inhabitants practice conservation—not because a bureaucrat tells them they should, but because the structure of property rights makes it in their own best interest to do so.

DISCUSSION QUESTIONS

1. Has there ever been a problem with the extinction of dogs, cats, or cattle? Why not?

2. Some argue that the only way to save rare species is to set up private game reserves to which wealthy hunters can travel. How could this help save endangered species? Do you see any parallels between this proposal and the CAMPFIRE program in Zimbabwe?

3. Is government *ownership* of animals needed to protect species from extinction?

4. In the United States, most fishing streams are public property, with access available to all. In Britain, most fishing streams are privately owned, with access restricted to those who are willing to pay for the right to fish. Anglers agree that over the past thirty years, the quality of fishing in the United States has declined, while the quality of fishing in Britain has risen. Can you suggest why?

25

Smog Merchants

Pollution is undesirable, almost by definition. Most of us use the term so commonly it suggests we all know, without question, what it means. Yet there is an important sense in which "pollution is what pollution does." Consider, for example, ozone (O_3), an unstable collection of oxygen atoms. At upper levels of the atmosphere it is a naturally occurring substance that plays an essential role in protecting life from the harmful effects of ultraviolet radiation. Without the ozone layer, skin cancer would likely become a leading cause of death, and spending a day at the beach would be as healthy as snuggling up to an open barrel of radioactive waste. At lower levels of the atmosphere, however, ozone occurs as a by-product of a chemical reaction between unburned hydrocarbons (as from petroleum products), nitrogen oxides, and sunlight.[1] In this form it is a major component of smog, and breathing it can cause coughing, asthma attacks, chest pain, and possibly long-term lung-function impairment.

Consider also polychlorinated biphenyls (PCBs), molecules that exist only in man-made form. Because they are chemically quite stable, PCBs are useful in a variety of industrial applications, including insulation in large electrical transformers. Without PCBs, electricity generation would be more expensive, as would the thousands of other goods that depend on electricity for their production and distribution. Yet PCBs are also highly toxic; acute exposure (e.g., from ingestion) can result in rapid death. Chronic (long-term)

---

[1] Ozone is also produced as a by-product of lightning strikes and other electrical discharges. Wherever and however it occurs, it has a distinctive metallic taste.

exposure is suspected to cause some forms of cancer. Illegal dumping of PCBs into streams and lakes has caused massive fish kills and is generally regarded as a threat to drinking-water supplies. And since PCBs are chemically stable (i.e., they decompose very slowly), once they are released into the environment they remain a potential threat for generations to come.

As these examples suggest, the notion of pollution is highly sensitive to context. Even crude oil, so essential as a source of energy, can become pollution when it appears on the shores of Alaska's pristine beaches. Despite this fact, we shall assume in what follows that (1) we all know what pollution is when we see, smell, taste, or even read about it, and (2) holding other things constant, less of it is preferred to more.

There are numerous ways to reduce or avoid pollution. Laws can be passed banning production processes that emit pollutants into the air and water or specifying minimum air- and water-quality levels or the maximum amount of pollution allowable. Firms would then be responsible for developing the technology and for paying the price to satisfy such standards. Or the law could specify the particular type of production technology to be used and the type of pollution-abatement equipment required in order to produce legally. Finally, subsidies could be paid to firms that reduce pollution emission, or taxes could be imposed on firms that engage in pollution emission.

No matter which methods are used to reduce pollution, costs will be incurred and problems will arise. For example, setting physical limits on the amount of pollution permitted would discourage firms from developing the technology that would reduce pollution beyond those limits. The alternative of subsidizing firms that reduce pollution levels may seem a strange use of taxpayers' dollars. The latest solution to the air pollution problem—selling or trading the rights to pollute—may seem even stranger. Nevertheless, this approach is now being used on a limited basis around the nation and on a much larger scale in Los Angeles, the smog capital of the country.

Under the plan that operates in the Los Angeles area, pollution allowances have been established for 390 of the area's largest polluters. Both nitrous oxide and sulphur dioxide, the two main ingredients of southern California's brown haze, are covered. Prior to the plan, which went into effect in 1994, the government told companies such as power plants and oil refineries what techniques they had to use to reduce pollutants. Under the new rules, companies are simply told how much they must reduce emissions each year, and they are then allowed to use whatever means they see fit to meet the standards. Over the initial ten years of the plan, firms will have their baseline emissions limits cut by 5 to 8 percent a year. By 2003, emissions of nitrous oxides from these sources should be down by 75 percent and sulphur dioxide by 60 percent.

The key element in the program is that the companies are allowed to buy and sell pollution rights. A firm that is successful in reducing pollutants below the levels to which it is entitled receives emission reduction credits (ERCs) for doing so. The firm can sell those credits to other firms, enabling the latter to exceed their baseline emissions by the amount of credits they purchase.

Presumably, firms that can cut pollutants in the lowest cost manner will do so, selling some of their credits to firms that find it more costly to meet the standards. Because the total level of emissions is determined ahead of time by the area's Air Quality Management District, the trading scheme will meet the requisite air quality standards. Yet because most of the emissions reductions will be made by firms that are the most efficient at doing so, the standards will be met at the lowest cost to society.

A similar market-based plan, covering only sulphur dioxide from selected sources, has been adopted by the Environmental Protection Agency (EPA) on a nationwide level. This program was kicked off by an auction of 150,000 air pollution allowances granted by the EPA. Each allowance permits a power utility to emit one ton of sulphur dioxide (SO_2) into the air. Based on their past records, utilities have been given rights to emit sulphur dioxide into the air at a declining rate into the future. By the year 2000, for example, utility emissions of sulphur dioxide had to be cut in half. Companies can either use their allowances to comply with the clean air regulations, or they can beat the standards and sell their unused allowances to other utilities.

As it turns out, although the EPA auctions probably helped get the trading process started, the expansion in private trades has been so rapid and extensive that the auctions are now a minor part of the market. Perhaps more importantly, the private market in allowances seems to be quite efficient at doing what it was designed to do—move allowances to their highest-valued locations, permit equalization of control costs across sources, and generate a key source of information about the costs of reducing SO_2 emissions.

Research conducted by Paul Joskow, Richard Schmalensee, and Elizabeth Bailey has found that after an initial twelve- to eighteen-month period in which there were few private trades and relatively high prices for the allowances—some $250 to $300 per ton—the market evolved rapidly.[2] By mid-1994 prices had dropped below $150 per ton and the volume of private trades exceeded the volume offered in the EPA auction. Since then, prices have fallen to about $100 per ton, and private trading of allowances for more than 5 million tons per year now dwarfs the EPA auction by a factor of 15 to 1.

This research also has uncovered two other quite important facts. First, the transaction costs of trading allowances are quite low—about 2 percent of the prevailing price. In addition, it appears that the prices at which trade takes place at any point in time are all quite close to one another. The spread between average bids and lowest winning bids at EPA auctions is only about 1 to 3 percent, and trading in the private market appears to be similarly concentrated around a single price at any point in time.

Because utilities can freely choose between either abating or emitting each ton of SO_2, they will only pay for an allowance what it will save them in abatement costs. Equivalently, a utility will pay no more for abatement than it would pay for an allowance to emit the SO_2. Thus, the existence of a common price for allowances assures us that the cost per ton of cutting emissions must be at that same level. That is, the costs of abating SO_2 emissions must be running about $100 per ton.

Perhaps not surprisingly, the notion of selling the right to pollute has been controversial, particularly among environmental organizations. The activist group Greenpeace, for example, claims that selling pollution allowances "is like giving a pack of cigarettes to a person dying of lung cancer." Nonetheless, other environmental groups have chosen to buy some of the allowances and retire them

---

[2] Paul L. Joskow, Richard Schmalensee, and Elizabeth M. Bailey, "The Market for Sulfur Dioxide Emissions," *American Economic Review*, September 1998, pp. 669–685.

unused. One such group was the Cleveland-based National Healthy Air License Exchange, whose president said, "It is our intent . . . to have a real effect on this market and on the quality of air."

Some observers have been disappointed that the government has taken so long to approve emissions-trading schemes. There appear to be two key reasons why progress has been so slow. First, many environmentalists are vigorously opposed to the very concept of tradable emissions, arguing that it amounts to putting a price on what traditionally has been considered a "priceless" resource—the environment. Because most of the cost savings that stem from tradable emissions-rights accrue to the polluters and their customers, government agencies have proceeded carefully, to avoid charges that they are somehow selling out to polluters.

Ironically, the second reason for the delay in developing markets for tradable pollution rights has been the reluctance on the part of industry to push harder for them. Similar programs in the past involved emissions credits that could be saved up (banked) by a firm for later use or bartered on a limited basis among firms. Under these earlier programs, environmental regulators would periodically wipe out emissions credits that firms thought they owned, on the ground that doing so provided a convenient means of preventing future environmental damage.

Not surprisingly, some companies believe that any credits purchased under a tradable-rights plan might be subject to the same sort of confiscation. Under such circumstances, firms have been understandably reluctant to support a program that might—or might not—prove to be of real value.[3] Indeed, even under the tradable-emissions plan adopted for Los Angeles, the regulators have explicitly stated that the emissions credits are *not* property rights and that they can be revoked at any time. Sadly, unless obstacles such as these can be removed, achieving environmental improvement at the lowest **social cost** is likely to remain a goal rather than an accomplishment.

---

[3] One can imagine the enthusiasm people would feel toward, say, the market for automobiles if the government announced that because cars were a source of pollution, the property rights to them might be revoked at any time, for any reason.

DISCUSSION QUESTIONS

1. Does marketing the right to pollute mean that we are allowing too much destruction of our environment?

2. Who implicitly has property rights to the air when the EPA auctions SO_2 permits? Does your answer depend on who gets the revenue raised by the auction?

3. Some environmental groups have opposed tradable pollution-rights on the grounds that this puts a price on the environment, when in fact the environment is a "priceless resource." Does this reasoning imply that we should be willing to give up *anything* (and therefore everything) to protect the environment? Does environmental quality have an infinite value? If not, how should we place a value on it?

4. Environmental regulations that prohibit emissions beyond some point implicitly allow firms and individuals to pollute up to that point at no charge. Don't such regulations amount to giving away environmental quality at no charge? Would it be better to charge a price via emissions taxes, for example, for the initial amount of pollutants? Would doing so reduce the amount of pollution?

26

Greenhouse Economics

The sky may not be falling, but it is getting warmer—maybe. The consequences will not be catastrophic, but they will be costly— maybe. We can reverse the process but should not spend very much to do so right now—maybe. Such is the state of the debate over the greenhouse effect—the apparent tendency of carbon dioxide (CO_2) and other gases to accumulate in the atmosphere, acting like a blanket that traps radiated heat, thereby increasing the earth's temperature. Before turning to the economics of the problem, let's take a brief look at the physical processes involved.

Certain gases in the atmosphere, chiefly water vapor and CO_2, trap heat radiating from the earth's surface. If they did not, the earth's average temperature would be roughly $0°F$ instead of just over $59°F$, and everything would be frozen solid. Human activity helps create some so-called greenhouse gases, including CO_2 (mainly from combustion of fossil fuels), methane (from crops and livestock), and chlorofluorocarbons (CFCs—from aerosol sprays, air conditioners, and refrigerators). We have the potential, unmatched in any other species, of profoundly altering our ecosystem.

There seems little doubt that humankind has been producing these gases at a record rate and that they are steadily accumulating in the atmosphere. Airborne concentrations of CO_2, for example, are increasing at the rate of about 0.5 percent per year; over the past 50 years, the amount of CO_2 in the atmosphere has risen a total of about 25 percent. Laboratory analysis of glacial ice dating back at least 160,000 years indicates that global temperatures and CO_2 levels in the atmosphere do, in fact, tend to move together, suggesting that the impact of today's rising CO_2 levels may be higher global temperatures in the future. Indeed, the National Academy of Sciences (NAS) has suggested that by the middle of the twenty-first century, greenhouse gases could be double the levels they were in 1860, and that global temperatures could rise by as much as 2° to 9°F.[1] The possible consequences of such a temperature increase include the following: a rise in the average sea level, inundating coastal areas, including most of Florida; the spread of algal blooms capable of deoxygenating major bodies of water, such as the Chesapeake Bay; and the conversion of much of the midwestern wheat and corn belt into a hot, arid dust bowl.

When an individual drives a car, heats a house, or uses an aerosol hair spray, greenhouse gases are produced. In economic terms, this creates a classic negative externality. Most of the costs (in this case, those arising from global warming) are borne by individuals *other than* the one making the decision about how many miles to drive or how much hair spray to use. Because the driver (or sprayer) enjoys all the benefits of the activity but suffers only a part of the cost, that individual engages in more than the economically efficient amount of the activity. In this sense, the problem of greenhouse gases parallels the problem that occurs when someone smokes a cigarette in an enclosed space or litters the countryside with fast-food wrappers. If we are to get individuals to reduce production of greenhouse gases to the efficient rate, we must somehow induce them to act *as though* they bear all the costs of their actions. The two most widely accepted means of doing this are government regulation and taxation, both of which have been proposed to deal with greenhouse gases.

The 1988 Toronto Conference on the Changing Atmosphere, attended by representatives from 48 nations, favored the regulation route. The Conference recommended a mandatory cut in CO_2 emissions by 2005 to 80 percent of their 1988 level—a move that would require a major reduction in worldwide economic output. The 1997 Kyoto conference on climate change, attended by representatives from 160 nations, made more specific but also more modest proposals. Overall, attendees agreed that by 2012, 38 developed nations

---

[1] This may not sound like much, but it does not take much to alter the world as we know it. The global average temperature at the height of the last ice age 18,000 years ago—when Canada and most of Europe were covered with ice—was 51°F, just 8° or so cooler than today.

should cut greenhouse emissions by 5 percent relative to 1990 levels. Developing nations, including China and India (the two most populous nations in the world), would be exempt from emissions cuts. On the taxation front, one prominent U.S. politician has proposed a tax of $100 per ton on the carbon emitted by fuels. It is estimated that such a tax would raise the price of coal by $70 per ton (about 300 percent) and elevate the price of oil by $8 per barrel, or about 40 percent. These proposals, and others like them, clearly have the potential to reduce the buildup of greenhouse gases but only at substantial costs. It thus makes some sense to ask: What are we likely to get for our money?

Perhaps surprisingly, the answer to this question is not obvious. Consider, for example, the raw facts of the matter. On average over the past century, greenhouse gases have been rising and so has the average global temperature. Yet most of the temperature rise occurred before 1940, whereas most of the increase in greenhouse gases has occurred after 1940. In fact, global average temperatures fell about 0.5°F between 1940 and 1970; this cooling actually led a number of prominent scientists during the 1970s to forecast a coming ice age!

Just as disconcerting is that the facts of global temperature change appear different depending on how and where temperature is measured. For example, if one looks only at ground-based measurements, the decade of the 1990s was clearly the warmest on record. Yet the upward trend in temperature that appears to hold true in these data is directly at odds with the results from other sources. Measurements taken using satellites and balloons, for example, suggest that there is *no* tendency for the average temperature of the atmosphere to rise. Why these discrepancies exist and what they mean for the future are issues still unresolved.

Nevertheless, let us suppose for the moment that, barring a significant reduction in greenhouse gas emissions, global warming is either under way or on the way. What can we expect? According to the most comprehensive study yet of this issue, a report by the prestigious National Academy of Sciences, the answer is a "good news, bad news" story.

The bad news is this: The likely rise in the sea level by one to three feet will inundate significant portions of our existing coastline; the expected decline in precipitation will necessitate more widespread use of irrigation; the higher average temperatures will compel more widespread use of air conditioning, along with the associated higher consumption of energy to power it; and the blazing heat in southern latitudes may make these areas too uncomfortable for all but the most heat-loving souls. The good news is that the technology for coping with changes such as these is well known and the costs of coping surprisingly small—on a scale measured in terms of hundreds of billions of dollars, of course. Moreover, many of the impacts that loom large at the individual level will represent much smaller costs at a societal level. For example, although higher average temperatures could prove disastrous for farmers in southern climes, the extra warmth could be an enormous windfall farther north, where year-round farming might become feasible. Similarly, the loss of shoreline due to rising sea levels would partly just be a migration of coastline inland—current beachfront property owners would suffer, but their inland neighbors would gain.[2]

None of these changes are free, of course, and there remain significant uncertainties about how global warming might affect species other than *Homo sapiens*. It is estimated, for example, that temperate forests can only "migrate" at a rate of about 100 kilometers per century, not fast enough to match the speed at which warming is expected to occur. Similarly, the anticipated rise in the sea level could wipe out between 30 and 70 percent of today's coastal wetlands. Whether new wetlands would develop along our new coastline and what might happen to species that occupy existing wetlands are issues that have not yet been resolved.

Yet the very uncertainties that surround the possible warming of the planet suggest that policy prescriptions of the sort that have been proposed—such as the cut in worldwide CO_2 emissions agreed to at Kyoto—may be too much, too soon. Indeed, the National Academy of Sciences recommended that we learn more before we leap too far. Caution seems particularly wise, because the exclusion of developing nations from any emissions cuts could result in huge costs for developed nations—and little or no reduction in worldwide greenhouse gases. Some sense of the damages that can be wrought by ignoring such counsel and rushing into a politically popular response to a

---

[2] There would be a net loss of land area and thus a net economic loss. Nevertheless, the net loss of land would be chiefly in the form of less valuable inshore property.

complex environmental issue is well illustrated by another atmospheric problem: smog.

Although gasoline is a major source of the hydrocarbons in urban air, its contribution to smog is plummeting because new cars are far cleaner than their predecessors. In the 1970s, cars spewed about 9 grams of hydrocarbons per mile; emissions controls brought this down to about 1.5 grams per mile by 1995. The cost of this reduction is estimated to be approximately $1000 for each ton of hydrocarbon emissions prevented—a number that many experts believe to be well below the benefits of the cleaner air that resulted. Despite the improvements in air quality, however, smog is still a significant problem in many major cities. Additional federal regulations aimed primarily at the nine smoggiest urban areas, including New York, Chicago, and Los Angeles, went into effect in 1995. Meeting these standards meant that gasoline had to be reformulated at a cost of about 6 cents per gallon. This brought the cost of removing each additional ton of hydrocarbons to about $10,000—some 10 times the per-ton cost of removing the first 95 percent from urban air.

Just as significantly, the 1995 EPA rules require that gasoline have a minimum oxygen content to help it burn. But because gasoline does not naturally contain oxygen, these rules effectively require refiners to put additives in their gas. At this point, there are only two additives that meet the EPA requirements: ethanol (refined from corn), and methyl tertiary butyl ether (MTBE). Because adding ethanol would drive the cost of gas up sharply, refiners have felt compelled to add MTBE. Yet MTBE has contaminated water supplies in California, and concern over its possible carcinogenic properties has led that state to seek a ban on its use as of 2003. A switch to ethanol is possible, of course. Yet the costs of doing so would far exceed those of the earlier gasoline reformulations—even though the EPA has never shown that the oxygen content requirement is necessary to meet its air quality standards. Although no one has yet come up with any estimate of benefits remotely close to costs such as these, we may well be stuck with enduring them, because few politicians want to be accused of being in favor of smog.

There is no doubt that atmospheric concentrations of greenhouse gases are rising and that human actions are the cause. It is probable that, as a result, the global average temperature is, or soon will be, rising. If temperatures do rise significantly, the costs will be large but the consequences are likely to be manageable. Given the nature of the problem, private action, taken on the individual level, will not yield the optimal outcome for society. Thus the potential gains from government action, in the form of environmental regulations or taxation, are substantial. But the key word here is *potential,* for government action, no matter how well intentioned, does not automatically yield benefits that exceed the costs. As we seek solutions to the potential problems associated with greenhouse gases, we must be sure that the consequences of action are not worse than those of first examining the problem further. If we forget this message, greenhouse economics may turn into bad economics—and worse policy.

DISCUSSION QUESTIONS

1. Why will voluntary actions, undertaken at the individual level, be unlikely to bring about significant reductions in greenhouse gases such as CO_2?

2. Does the fact that the CO_2 produced in one nation results in adverse effects on other nations have any bearing on the likelihood that CO_2 emissions will be reduced to the optimal level? Would the problem be easier to solve if all the costs and benefits were concentrated within a single country? Within a single elevator?

3. The policy approach to greenhouse gases will almost certainly involve limits on emissions, rather than taxes on emissions. Can you suggest why limits rather than taxes are likely to be used?

4. It costs about $80,000 per acre to create wetlands. How reasonable is this number as an estimate of what wetlands are worth?

27

The Economics of Weather Forecasting

Every government action has costs and generates benefits. Figuring out which of these—the costs or the benefits—is bigger in any given situation is often problematic. Data on the cost side usually are not too difficult to establish. After all, the direct budgetary costs typically are a matter of public record, and economists have developed a variety of ways to convert these budgetary data into numbers that correspond fairly closely with the relevant economic concepts of cost.

The real trouble comes when we try to determine the benefits of government action. For example, what is the economic benefit of having an antiballistic missile system, or the U.S. State Department, or, for that matter, the Weather Service? Surely these things are valuable, but just as surely, as with many things the government does, there is no marketplace that helps us in establishing what people are willing to pay for such services. In cases such as these, the government is producing services that are (or are close to being) public goods. This means that the goods have two characteristics. First, the consumption of the goods is nonrivalrous: the quantity available for you to consume does not fall when we consume more. An antiballistic missile system, for example, simultaneously can protect us all. Second, the consumption of these goods is (or is close to being) nonexcludable: it is extremely costly to provide the goods only to people who pay for them, while at the same time preventing or excluding nonpayers from obtaining them. Thus, even if you refuse to pay for the missile system, it continues to protect you from attack.

The nonexcludable aspect of public goods makes it difficult to get the private sector interested in providing these goods, because it is so hard to make a profit from them. This in turn means that either the government gets involved, or the good doesn't get produced at all. But because there is no market—and thus no market prices—for such goods, it is difficult to properly value them to compute the benefits of having the government provide them.

Every once in awhile, however, it is possible to estimate these benefits through fairly ingenious indirect means. Erik Craft of the University of Richmond has done just that in studying the first twenty years of what was to become the modern-day U.S. Weather Service.[1] He concludes that the agency's collection of weather data and the dissemination of storm warnings across the Great Lakes region did in fact yield substantial, positive net benefits to society. These benefits came in terms of both averted economic losses due to shipwrecks, and fewer lives lost at sea.

The U.S. Congress established a national weather organization in 1870 when it instructed the Secretary of War to collect meteorological observations and issue storm warnings on the Great Lakes. If severe weather forecasts were a valuable transportation input, one would expect several consequences after the service was introduced in the early 1870s. Specifically, the collection and dissemination of weather information should have caused a clearly measurable decline in shipping losses on the Great Lakes. This also should have manifested itself in predictable changes in shipping rates and insurance premiums. Because fall weather on the Great Lakes is considerably more turbulent and destructive than summer weather, the beneficial impact of the storm warning system should have been much greater in the fall than in the summer.

---

[1] Erik D. Craft, "The Value of Weather Information Services for Nineteenth-Century Great Lakes Shipping," *American Economic Review* v. 88 no. 5, pp. 1059–1076, December 1998. Strictly speaking, weather information today probably only satisfies the first criterion (nonrivalrous consumption) for being a public good. With today's technology for encrypting data, it is entirely possible to exclude nonpayers from consuming weather information, and there is indeed a large market in privately produced weather forecasts purchased by airlines, ocean shipping companies, and interstate truckers. But 130 years ago, before the advent of wireless radio, it was far more difficult to exclude nonpayers from weather forecasts made for ships: the forecasts were broadcast by means of shore-based flags and semaphores visible to everyone.

After controlling for a host of other factors that might influence the analysis—including year-to-year fluctuations in weather conditions and the transition from sail to steam power during this period—Craft found clear evidence that storm warnings sharply reduced the incidence of shipping losses on the Great Lakes. Measured in terms of today's dollars, the storm warning system as a whole generated benefits of $20 million per year during the early years, rising to nearly $90 million per year during the late 1880s, the end of the study period. These benefits, resulting from fewer shipwrecks and reduced cargo losses, were achieved at an annual cost of under $20 million per year. It also appears that the storm warning system played a key role in saving fifty to seventy seamen's lives annually during this period, a benefit on top of the reduced shipping and cargo losses.

Given that establishing the Weather Service led to significant declines in shipping losses, the result should have been lower costs for firms offering shipping services, and also for companies insuring the ships and their cargo. Because the storm warning information was much more useful during stormy fall months, the differences between insurance and shipping rates in the peaceful summer months and the turbulent fall months should have diminished. The evidence is consistent with these predictions. The fall shipping price premium shrank by 50 percent due to the storm warning stations, and the ratio of fall-to-summer insurance premiums declined as well. Overall, the social rate of return from the expenditures on weather collection and dissemination during this period was at least 64 percent.

A one-year reduction in the Army Signal Service budget in fiscal year 1883 due to an embezzlement scandal conveniently provided an additional means of discerning the beneficial effects of the Weather Service. The budget cut forced a temporary reduction in the number of storm warning stations by nearly one-half. The result was a natural experiment: The apparently beneficial effects of the Weather Service should have been sharply curtailed during the period of budget austerity, only to return to their former levels with the restoration of the agency's full funding. This was precisely the pattern observed.

The 1883 budget cut saved about $2.5 million. But shipping losses that year soared from $30 million to about $55 million, returning to about $30 million when the funding was restored.

Moreover, it appears that the sharp rise in shipping losses was accompanied by a corresponding increase in fatalities.

None of this evidence means, of course, that the timing of the establishment of the Weather Service was necessarily optimal. Nor does it imply that the government provision of weather information was necessary. Indeed, at the time the U.S. Weather Service was launched, one entrepreneur had already begun organizing the resources necessary to offer privately provided storm warnings to Great Lakes shipping companies. In fact, the scientist he was going to use as chief meteorologist was the man tapped to head the government effort. Once the government began offering storm warnings at no direct charge to shipping companies or insurers, the private effort collapsed. Today, although the National Weather Service offers its forecasts at no charge, there are many private weather forecasting services that profit handsomely by providing (presumably superior) forecasts to a host of consumers, including agribusinesses, airlines, America's Cup sailing teams, power utilities, ski areas, and trucking companies, to name but a few.

Whether private-sector weather forecasting and storm warnings could have beaten government's performance in protecting Great Lakes shipping during the eighteenth century is unknown. But in a world in which it seems all too easy to find examples of the waste generated by government policies, it is of some comfort to find an episode in which the government contributed positively to the well-being of the public it is supposed to serve.

DISCUSSION QUESTIONS

1. Consumption of many goods, including television shows and sporting events, is nonrivalrous, in the sense that when one person enjoys the performance it does not diminish the quantity or quality of performance available for others to consume. What makes it feasible for such goods to be provided by the private sector?

2. Consider a good the consumption of which is rivalrous, but which is nonexcludable. For example, suppose the government made it illegal for apartment owners to exclude (by charging a positive monthly rental) people from living in their apartments. Do you think apartments would continue to be provided by the private sector? Do the answers to this and question 1 reveal whether it is the rivalrous or the excludable features of goods that determine whether the private sector is able to profitably supply them?

3. Suppose that the job done by the U.S. Weather Service in the late eighteenth century was actually inferior to the job that would have been done by a private-sector firm. Is it still possible that the private-sector firm would find it impossible to compete against the Weather Service? Is it possible that ship owners might prefer the inferior government service over the superior private service?

4. The next time you see a sporting event on television, watch carefully for an announcement specifying restrictions on your rights to rebroadcast the event or distribute it commercially. Why are these restrictions imposed on you and other viewers? What would be the likely consequences if the government prohibited sports leagues from imposing such restrictions?

28

Property Rights and Forests

Recent estimates are that the world's forests are shrinking at about 1 percent per year. At this rate, the extent of the globe's forest lands will be cut in *half* during your lifetime. Because of the important ecological functions performed by forests, including the removal of carbon dioxide from the atmosphere, the consequences for the world's ecological balance may be staggering.

Most discussions of forest losses depict private parties—chiefly, logging companies—as trying to harvest trees as quickly as they can, without regard for the current or future consequences of their actions. Hence, it is said, only government action can prevent the loss of the world's forests. These discussions cast the impending deforestation of South and Central America, Southeast Asia, and Africa as a classic example of the need to rely on the government to protect the environment from the ravages of free enterprise.

But there is growing evidence that the government's failure to define and enforce secure property rights is also a key element of the problem. In a series of papers, Robert Deacon of the University of California, Santa Barbara, has evaluated the role of secure property rights in preventing forest loss around the world. Examining both the long-term historical record and contemporary data, Deacon has found that secure property rights, usually the result of stable, democratic political systems, play a crucial role in slowing the rate at which forests are harvested. This in turn implies that secure property rights are an essential ingredient in preserving and enhancing the quality of the global environment.

Insecure property rights cause deforestation in a variety of ways. Directly, the absence of secure ownership induces both trespassers and forest owners (who cannot defend their own property) to cut timber sooner and not to replant after forests are cleared. In effect, harvesting is the only way to obtain property rights, and few people will replant, fearing that someone else will harvest first. On both counts, forest lands can quickly degenerate into wasteland. Indirectly, the absence of secure property rights threatens forests by deterring agricultural investments in irrigation, terracing, and soil enrichment. By reducing agricultural yields, the failure to invest forces the clearing of more land to make up for the loss of food output. (An interesting side note to this is that pesticides and fertilizers used in agriculture can actually protect forests by improving crop yields and so reduce the amount of land that must be cleared.)

In the pre-Christian Roman Empire, ancient Greece, and elsewhere, clearly defined and well-enforced property rights served to protect forests. But as these civilizations declined, property rights in forests were weakened. The result was over-harvesting, inadequate reforestation, and thus substantial deforestation. In more recent times, the forests of France suffered extensively in the chaos that followed the French Revolution, as did the forests of Greece after that nation's War of Independence in 1821. In this century, the forests of Europe were devastated during World War II, not only by war damage, but also by destructive cutting by civilians and lack of reforestation. Similar damage occurred to forests in Java during the turmoil that followed the end of Dutch colonial rule after World War II.

Around the world today, clear measures of political instability and insecure property rights are associated with more rapid deforestation. For example, nations such as Lebanon, Haiti, and El Salvador, torn by major constitutional changes, guerilla warfare, or frequent regime changes, tend to suffer heavier forest losses. By contrast, countries with democratically elected legislatures and stable, civilian governments, such as Western European and North American nations, tend to have both lower harvesting rates and higher reforestation rates. In addition, the security of property rights stimulates agricultural investment, thereby increasing agricultural yields, which further reduces deforestation. Overall, the existence of stable, democratic governments and rule by law rather than by individuals play a central role in protecting the world's forests. This helps explain why forests in the United States and much of Europe are actually *growing* in size, even though they are shrinking elsewhere.

The importance of property rights in getting the maximum economic and environmental benefits from our forests is also clear when we examine government-owned and -operated forests in the United States. Don Leal of the Political Economy Research Center (PERC), for example, has compared the performance of forest management practices on forests owned by state governments with those operated by the U.S. Forest Service.[1] In a variety of states, including Montana and Minnesota, Leal has assessed the relative economic and environmental performance of forests managed by state government employees versus those managed by federal government employees. He reaches two conclusions. First, the forests managed by state governments produce superior economic performance relative to otherwise comparable forests managed by the federal government. Second, this superior economic performance is achieved with higher environmental quality in the state-managed lands. How can both of these outcomes be true at the same time? The answer, it seems, is property rights.

By congressional mandate, national forests are managed to achieve the "combination [of land uses] that will best meet the needs of the America people...." As you might imagine, this vague directive gives no real direction to the U.S. Forest Service employees who manage the national forests: Almost any set of economic or environmental outcomes is consistent with this mandate, which means that almost any degree of economic waste or environmental degradation fulfills Congress's directive.

In contrast, state law in Montana mandates that the state's forests be managed to provide funding for public schools. In Minnesota, the revenue from state forests goes into the treasuries of local governments. It is important that in both cases, the net revenues from logging operations (timber sales revenues minus harvesting costs) are effectively owned by clearly defined con-

---

[1] Donald R. Leal, "Turning a Profit on Public Forests," *PERC Policy Series PS-4,* September 1995.

stituencies—public schools in one case and local governments in the other. By contrast, revenues from national forests simply go into the U.S. Treasury, where no clearly identifiable group has claim to them. The impact of this difference in property rights is dramatic. State forests generate considerably more net revenue from timber management than do national forests: In Montana, state forests yield $2.00 in revenue for every dollar of costs, while adjacent national forests yield only $0.80 in revenue for each dollar of costs. In Minnesota, state forests generate $1.70 in revenue per dollar of costs, while federal forests yield but $0.50 in revenue per dollar of costs. Leal's colleague Holly Fretwell has found that these results are no fluke. When she combines the Montana data with evidence from forests in Washington, Idaho, and Oregon, the numbers are even more dramatic. Federally managed forests yield $0.76 in revenue for each dollar of costs, while state-managed forests yield $5.62 in revenue for each dollar in costs—an eightfold performance margin for the state-managed lands.

The strikingly superior economic performance of state forests is due mostly to the lower costs that states incur in managing their lands. Although revenues are slightly higher from state forests, chiefly because of less clear-cutting and more selective cutting on state lands, the key factor is that forest managers—directly under the scrutiny of local citizens who have a stake in the forests—simply use much fewer resources in managing their forests. Notably, labor costs on the state lands are 30 to 50 percent lower than they are on the federal properties.

It might be thought that these lower costs are the result of stinting on environmental protection on state lands. In fact, just the *reverse* appears to be true: Evaluations conducted by independent assessment boards (which included state and federal officials and environmental groups) reveal that environmental protection and environmental quality are both *greater* on the state lands than on the federal properties. Not only is clear-cutting less prevalent on state lands, environmental protection procedures on state lands are more effective in protecting wildlife habitat, water quality, and other measures of environmen tal quality.

We now see that a growing body of research points to the truly productive role of government in protecting and enhancing the productivity of forests. Well-defined, secure private property rights discourage deforestation because potential harvesters will allow trees to grow longer, secure that the mature timber will be safe, and they will be more likely to replant, confident that they or their descendants will reap the benefits. Moreover, the benefits we derive from government-owned forests—both economic and environmental—are substantially enhanced when property rights to those benefits reside with clearly identifiable groups or individuals.

A principal cause of shrinking forests is the lack of secure private ownership, and a principal cause of forest mismanagement is a failure to clearly define any property rights. Viewed in this light, the way to reduce wasteful deforestation and the wasteful use of our existing forests is to work toward the establishment of secure, enforceable rights to forests. This in turn will yield the greatest protection for and the most productive use of the forests—in the present and the future.

DISCUSSION QUESTIONS

1. Imagine two groups of individuals, each with a gallon of fresh popcorn in front of it. For one group, all of the popcorn is in a single communal bowl, and people can remove popcorn from the bowl only to eat it. For the other group, the popcorn is divided up into separate bowls, one bowl for each individual; a person wishing to consume popcorn may take it only out of his or her own bowl. In which group will the popcorn be consumed the fastest?

2. Suppose the popcorn in question 1 can be replenished from some other source, but only at the expense of time and other resources by the person doing the replenishment. Further suppose that any replenishment popcorn is subject to the same rules as the original popcorn: It goes into the common bowl of the first group, or into the individual bowl of the replenisher in the second group. For which group is replenishment more likely?

3. Suppose that in the case of state-owned forests, the net revenues from harvesting timber went into the states' general

revenue funds, rather than being earmarked for public schools. How would this likely affect oversight of the forest management agencies in the states? What impact would this likely have on the *costs* of harvesting?

4. Is it possible for forests to be harvested too *infrequently*? Is it possible to have too *much* land devoted to forests, rather than to farmland or suburbs?

Part Seven

The International Scene

INTRODUCTION

As we enter the twenty-first century, an increasing number of the public issues we face are international in character. This is as it should be, for the rapid developments in information processing, communications, and transportation over the past twenty-five years are gradually knitting the economies of the world closer together. Political developments, most notably the dismantling of the Iron Curtain and the dissolution of the Soviet Union, have contributed to this growing economic integration.

As we see in Chapter 29, "The Benefits of Free Trade," these developments offer both the prospects of great gain and the risk of substantial losses. The passage of the North American Free Trade Agreement (NAFTA) and the creation of the World Trade Organization (WTO) have substantially reduced the barriers to trade between the United States and most of the rest of the world. If we take advantage of these lower trade barriers, we have the opportunity to make ourselves far better off by specializing in those activities in which we have a **comparative advantage** and then trading the fruits of our efforts with other nations.

Because voluntary exchange also often redistributes wealth, in addition to creating it, there will always be some individuals who oppose free trade. There are many smokescreens behind which the self-interested opposition to free trade is hidden, as we see in Chapter 30, "The Opposition to Free Trade." Nevertheless, although

protectionism—the creation of trade barriers such as tariffs and quotas—often sounds sensible, it is in fact a surefire way to reduce rather than enhance our wealth. If we ignore the value of free trade, we do so only at our own peril.

To illustrate the tremendous damages that can be wrought when protectionism gains the upper hand, Chapter 31, "The $750,000 Job," examines what happens when tariffs and quotas are imposed in an effort to "save" U.S. jobs from foreign competition. The sad facts are that (1) in the long run, it is almost impossible to effectively protect U.S. workers from foreign competition, and (2) efforts to do so not only reduce Americans' overall living standards, but they also end up costing the jobs of other Americans. The moral of our story is that competition is just as beneficial on the international scene as it is on the domestic front.

Indeed, the enormous gains that accrue from mutually beneficial exchange create forces that are generally beyond the powers of any subset of individuals—or even governments—to master. What is true for drugs, abortion, water, and apartments is just as true for goods traded internationally. Politicians may pass legislation, and bureaucrats may do their best to enforce it, but the laws of demand and supply ultimately rule the economy—even when that economy encompasses the entire world.

29

The Benefits of Free Trade

The decade of the 1990s was a time of great change on the international trade front. The North American Free Trade Agreement (NAFTA), for example, substantially reduced the barriers to trade among citizens of Canada, the United States, and Mexico. On a global scale, the Uruguay round of the General Agreement on Tariffs and Trade (GATT) was ratified by 117 nations including the United States. Under the terms of this agreement, GATT was replaced by the now 132-member World Trade Organization (WTO), and **tariffs** were cut worldwide. Agricultural **subsidies** were reduced, patent protections were extended, and the WTO is establishing a set of arbitration boards to settle international disputes over trade issues.

Many economists believe that both NAFTA and the agreements reached during the Uruguay round were victories not only for free trade but also for the citizens of the participating nations. Nevertheless, many noneconomists, particularly politicians, opposed these agreements, so it is important we understand what is beneficial about NAFTA, the WTO, and free trade in general.

Voluntary trade creates new wealth. In voluntary trade, both parties in an exchange gain. They give up something of lesser value in return for something of greater value. In this sense, exchanges are always unequal. But it is this unequal nature of exchange that is the source of the increased productivity and higher wealth that occurs whenever trade takes place. When we engage in exchange, what we give up is worth less than what we get—for if this were not true, we would not have traded. And what is true for us is also true for our trading partner, meaning that partner is better off too.

Free trade encourages individuals to employ their talents and abilities in the most productive manner possible and to exchange the fruits of their efforts. The **gains from trade** lie in one of the most fundamental ideas in economics—a nation gains from doing what it can do best relative to other nations, that is, by specializing in those endeavors in which it has a comparative advantage. Trade encourages individuals and nations to discover ways to specialize so that they can become more productive and enjoy higher incomes. Increased productivity and the subsequent increase in the rate of economic growth are exactly what the members of the WTO round and NAFTA sought—and are obtaining—by reducing trade barriers.

To see the principle of comparative advantage in a concrete example, suppose you and your roommate wish to divide the responsibilities associated with your living arrangements. There are two activities that must be performed: household duties, such as cleaning, cooking, and yard work; and marketplace duties, that is, earning enough income to pay for the rent, utilities, and food. Suppose that if you spend all your time each week performing household services, you can produce one unit, whereas if you spend all your time in the marketplace, you can earn $500 per week. To complete the description of your activities, imagine that all linear combinations of these extremes are possible: Thus by splitting your time equally between the two activities you could simultaneously produce one half-unit of household services while also earning $250 in the market.

Now suppose your roommate is somewhat younger and less experienced than you and so is less productive in the market. That is, your roommate can also produce one unit of household services if he or she spends the entire week at it but can only earn $300 per week in the market. Finally, if your roommate divides time equally between the two activities, one half of the housework will get done at the same time that he or she can earn $150 in market work. Now we want to consider how you and your roommate should go about your weekly activities.

To keep things simple, we shall assume you both agree that exactly one unit of household services is just enough to keep the household clean, the meals cooked, and the yard tidy. Thus you must decide how this unit is to be produced. Presumably, in deciding this, it is important to know how much time will be left over for market services, for it is income from the market that enables you to pay your bills.

One possible arrangement is for both of you to be self-sufficient: That is, each of you does one half of the household services and then spends the rest of your time in the marketplace. This will leave your roommate with time to earn $150. For your part, when you do half of the household chores, you have enough time left over to earn $250 in producing market services. Thus total household income is $400 and all of the housework gets done.

But there is another possibility: Although your roommate appears to be no better than you at housekeeping, your roommate in fact has a comparative advantage at producing household services, being able to produce them at lower cost than you can. Specifically, the half-unit of housekeeping produced by your roommate costs only $150. The half-unit produced by you is done at an opportunity cost of $250, because this is the amount of market income you sacrifice. We say that your roommate is the low-cost provider of household services, whereas you are the low-cost producer of market services. Hence, you can *both* gain if your roommate specializes in housekeeping (producing the desired one unit), while you specialize in market services, earning $500. You can then engage in exchange with your roommate, handing over, say, $200 in return for the household services you receive, leaving you with $300 for other goods. The net result is that all of the household services continue to get produced, and you both end up with more income to spend.

The important feature of this example is that it summarizes the essence of all trading arrangements and demonstrates why voluntary exchange is generally superior to self-sufficiency. Exchange is productive because it permits individuals (and nations) to specialize in those activities they can perform at lower cost. This conserves resources, or equivalently, enables more total output to be produced from the same initial amount of resources.

Note particularly that it is *exchange* between you and your roommate that permits you both to specialize and thus raises your combined income by $100. Without exchange (or trade) your roommate would not be willing to keep house only, for this would lead to starvation. In effect, the exchange between the two of you literally produced $100 worth of income, because only via exchange could this extra income be achieved.

Because trade—at the individual or the national level—typically does result in both parties being better off, we say that trade is a **positive sum game**. That is, it is an activity that makes a positive contribution to wealth. Indeed, it is this feature of trade that induces individuals to voluntarily engage in it. It is also the reason that nations trade with each other.

It is easy to see this in our example of you and your roommate, and it probably even makes intuitive sense regarding trade between and among the fifty states in the union. Why would it no longer be true simply because foreigners are involved? International trade, too, is a positive sum game. Thus even though England and America are both capable of producing both grain and beer, we import beer from England, exporting grain to pay for it. The pattern of trade is in this direction because America has a comparative advantage in grain production, whereas England's comparative advantage lies in beer production. By taking advantage of the differences in production costs in the two nations, the residents of both are made better off—their wealth is raised.

Note something else about these exchanges. When you trade with your roommate, what is valuable to you in the deal is the housekeeping services you receive. The cash you hand over to your roommate is the cost to you of the trade. In international trade parlance, you are importing housekeeping services and exporting market services to pay for those imports. Similarly, America is importing beer in return for the grain it exports to pay for it. In both cases, imports are the benefits of trade, whereas exports are the costs that must be incurred because our trading partners insist on being paid for their efforts.

There is one last point: Throughout this entire process, you and your roommate were working full time—both when you were self-sufficient and when you were specialized and engaged in trade. Note particularly that neither of you became unemployed as a result of trade—you simply worked in different employments and enjoyed higher wealth for doing so. Exactly the same sort of pattern applies to trade between England and America. Because they engage in trade, people in England are more likely to produce beer than otherwise, whereas Americans are more likely to produce grain than otherwise. But in both countries, people are fully employed before and after. The difference is that when they trade they get paid more for their work.

Trade is beneficial: It conserves resources and raises our wealth. This is why arrangements such as NAFTA and the WTO are beneficial for Americans and for the residents of nations with whom America trades. Despite this fact, many governments, including the American government, often impose regulations or pass laws that prohibit or restrict trade. Why such behavior occurs is the subject of our next chapter.

DISCUSSION QUESTIONS

1. What effect would a U.S. import tariff (that is, a tax on each unit of imported goods) have on the amount of goods imported into the United States?

2. What effect would a U.S. import tariff have on U.S. *exports* of goods?

3. The U.S. government currently restricts the export of oil from Alaska to foreign countries. What effect does this have on American *imports*?

4. Is it ever possible for the imposition of an import tariff by the United States to make citizens of the United States better off?

30

The Opposition to Free Trade

Voluntary trade—between individuals or nations—raises the wealth of both trading parties. As we saw in Chapter 29, there are two reasons for this. First, trade moves goods from lower-valued uses to higher-valued uses, enabling the trading partners to share the rise in value that results. Second, voluntary exchange permits economic agents to specialize in producing those goods in which they have a comparative advantage, that is, the goods for which they are low-cost producers. This permits more efficient—and thus more productive—use of our scarce resources.

Despite these gains from exchange, free trade is routinely opposed by some (and sometimes many) people, particularly in the case of international trade. There are many excuses offered for this opposition, but they all basically come down to one issue. When our borders are open to trade with other nations, some individuals and businesses within our nation face more competition. As we saw in Chapter 17, most firms and workers hate competition, and who can blame them? After all, if a firm can keep the competition out, profits are sure to rise. And if workers can prevent competition from other sources, they can enjoy higher wages and greater selection among jobs. So the real source of most opposition to international trade is that the opponents to trade dislike the competition that comes with it. There is nothing immoral or unethical about this—but there is nothing altruistic or noble about this, either. It is self-interest, pure and simple.

Opposition to free trade is, of course, nothing new on the American landscape. In this century, one of the most famous examples of such opposition resulted in the Smoot-Hawley Tariff of 1930. This major federal government statute was a classic example of protectionism—an effort to protect a subset of American producers at the expense of consumers and other producers. It included tariff schedules for over 20,000 products, raising taxes on affected imports by an average of 52 percent.

The Smoot-Hawley Tariff encouraged beggar-thy-neighbor policies by the rest of the world. Such policies represent an attempt to improve (a portion of) one's domestic economy at the expense of foreign countries' economies. In this case, tariffs were imposed to discourage imports, in order that domestic import-competing industries would benefit. The beggar-thy-neighbor policy at the heart of the Smoot-Hawley Tariff Act of 1930 was soon adopted by the United Kingdom, France, the Netherlands, and Switzerland. The result was a massive reduction in international trade. According to many economists, this caused a worsening of the ongoing worldwide depression of the period.

Opponents of free trade sometimes claim that beggar-thy-neighbor policies benefit the United States by protecting import-competing industries. In general, this claim is not correct. It is true that some Americans benefit from such policies, but two large groups of Americans lose. First, there are the purchasers of imports and import-competing goods. They suffer from higher prices and reduced selection of goods and suppliers caused by tariffs and import **quotas**. Second, the decline in imports caused by protectionism also causes a decline in exports, thereby harming firms and employees in these industries. This follows directly from one of the most fundamental propositions in international trade: *In the long run, imports are paid for by exports.* This proposition simply states that when one country buys goods and services from the rest of the world (imports), the rest of the world eventually wants goods from that country (exports) in exchange. Given this fundamental proposition, a corollary becomes obvious: *Any restriction on imports leads to a reduction in exports.* Thus any business for import-competing industries gained as a result of tariffs or quotas means at least as much business *lost* for exporting industries.

Opponents to free trade often raise a variety of objections in their efforts to restrict it. For example, it is sometimes claimed that foreign companies engage in dumping, that is, selling their goods in America below cost. The first question to ask when such charges are made is this: Below *whose* cost? Clearly, if the foreign firm is selling in America, it must be offering the good for sale at a price that is at or below the costs of American firms, or else it could not induce

Americans to buy it. But the ability of individuals or firms to get goods at lower cost is in fact one of the *benefits* of free trade, not one of its damaging features.

What about claims that import sales are taking place at prices below the *foreign* company's costs? This amounts to arguing that the owners of the foreign company are voluntarily giving some of their wealth to us, namely, the difference between their costs and the (lower) price they charge us. It is possible, though unlikely, they might wish to do this, perhaps because this could be the cheapest way of getting us to try a product that we would not otherwise purchase. But even supposing it is true, why would we want to refuse this gift? As a nation, we are richer if we accept it. Moreover, it is a gift that will be offered only in the short run: There is no point in selling at below cost unless one hopes to soon raise price profitably above cost!

Another argument sometimes raised against international trade is that the goods are produced abroad using unfair labor practices (such as the use of child labor) or using production processes that do not meet American environmental standards. It is surely the case that such charges are sometimes correctly levied. But we must remember two things here. First, although we may find the use of child labor (or perhaps sixty-hour weeks with no overtime pay) objectionable, such practices were at one time commonplace in the United States. They used to be engaged in here for the same reason they are currently practiced abroad: The people involved were (or are) too poor to do otherwise. Some families in developing nations literally cannot survive unless all members of their family contribute. As unfortunate as this is, if we insist on imposing our tastes—shaped in part by our extraordinarily high wealth—on peoples whose wealth is far lower than ours, we run the risk of making them worse off even as we think we are helping them.

Similar considerations apply to environmental standards.[1] It is well established that individuals' and nations' willingness to pay for environmental quality is very much shaped by their wealth: Environmental quality is a luxury good; that is, people who are rich (such as Americans) want to consume much more of it per capita than do people who are poor. Insisting that other nations meet environmental standards that we find acceptable is much like insisting that they wear

---

[1] There is one important exception to this argument. In the case of foreign air or water pollution generated near enough to our borders (for example with Mexico or Canada) to cause harm to Americans, good public policy presumably dictates that we seek to treat such pollution as though it were being generated inside our borders.

the clothes we wear, use the modes of transportation we prefer, and consume the foods we like. The few people who manage to afford it will indeed be living in the style to which we are accustomed, but most people will not be able to afford much of anything.

Our point is not that foreign labor or environmental standards are, or should be, irrelevant to Americans. Our point instead is that achieving high standards of either is costly, and trade restrictions are unlikely to be the most efficient or effective way to achieve them. Just as importantly, labor standards and environmental standards are all too often raised as smokescreens to hide the real motive: keeping the competition out.

If it is true that free trade is beneficial and that restrictions on trade generally are harmful, we must surely raise the question: How does legislation like the Smoot-Hawley Tariff (or any other trade restriction) ever get passed? As Mark Twain noted many years ago, the reason the free traders win the arguments and the protectionists win the votes is this: Foreign competition often clearly affects a narrow and specific import-competing industry such as textiles, shoes, or automobiles, and thus trade restrictions benefit a narrow, well-defined group of economic agents. For example, restrictions on imports of Japanese automobile imports in the 1980s chiefly benefited the Big Three automakers in this country: General Motors, Ford, and Chrysler. Similarly, long-standing quotas on the imports of sugar benefit a handful of large American sugar producers. Because of the concentrated benefits that accrue when Congress votes in favor of trade restrictions, sufficient monies can be raised in those industries to convince members of Congress to impose those restrictions.

The eventual reduction in exports that must follow is normally spread in small doses throughout all export industries. Thus no specific group of workers, managers, or shareholders in export industries will feel that it should contribute money to convince Congress to reduce international trade restrictions. Additionally, although consumers of imports and import-competing goods lose due to trade restrictions, they too are typically a diffuse group of individuals, none of whom individually will be affected a great deal because of any single import restriction. It is the simultaneous existence of concentrated benefits and diffuse costs that led to Mark Twain's conclusion that the protectionists would often win the votes.

Of course the protectionists don't win all the votes—after all, about one-eighth of the American economy is based on international trade. Despite the opposition to free trade that comes from many quarters, its benefits to the economy as a whole are so great it is unthinkable that we might do away with international trade altogether. Thus, when we think about developments such as the North American Free Trade Agreement (NAFTA) and the World Trade Organization (WTO), it is clear that both economic theory and empirical evidence indicate that, on balance, Americans will be better off after—and because of—the move to freer trade.

DISCUSSION QUESTIONS

1. During the late 1980s and early 1990s, American automobile manufacturers greatly increased the quality of the cars they produced, relative to the quality of the cars produced in other nations. What effect do you think this had on (1) American imports of Japanese cars, (2) Japanese imports of American cars, and (3) American exports of goods and services other than automobiles?

2. Over the last fifteen years, some Japanese automakers have opened plants in the United States so that they could produce (and sell) "Japanese" cars in the United States. What effect do you think this had on (1) American imports of Japanese cars, (2) Japanese imports of American cars, and (3) American exports of goods and services other than automobiles?

3. For a number of years, Japanese carmakers voluntarily limited the number of cars they exported to the United States. What effect do you think this had on (1) Japanese imports of American cars, and (2) American exports of goods and services other than automobiles?

4. Until recently, American cars exported to Japan had driver controls on the left side of the car (as in America) even though the Japanese drive on the left side of the road, and thus Japanese cars sold in Japan have driver controls on the right side. Suppose the Japanese tried to sell their cars in America with the driver controls on the right side. What impact would this likely have on their sales in this country? Do you think the unwillingness of American carmakers to put the driver controls on the correct side for exports to Japan had any effect on their sales of cars in that country?

31

The $750,000 Job

In even-numbered years, particularly years evenly divisible by four, politicians of all persuasions are apt to give long-winded speeches about the need to protect U.S. jobs from the evils of foreign competition. To accomplish this goal, we are encouraged to buy American. If further encouragement is needed, we are told that if we do not voluntarily reduce the amount of imported goods we purchase, the government will impose (or make more onerous) either tariffs (taxes) on imported goods or quotas (quantity restrictions) that physically limit imports. The objective of this exercise is to save U.S. jobs.

Unlike black rhinos or blue whales, U.S. jobs are in no danger of becoming extinct. There are an infinite number of potential jobs in the American economy, and there always will be. Some of these jobs are not very pleasant, and many others do not pay very well, but there will always be employment of some sort as long as there is scarcity. Thus when an autoworker making $45,000 per year says that imports of Japanese cars should be reduced to save his job, what he really means is this: He wants to be protected from competition so that he can continue his present employment at the same or higher salary, rather than move to a different employment that has less desirable working conditions or pays a lower salary. There is nothing wrong with the autoworker's goal (better working conditions and higher pay), but it has nothing to do with saving jobs. (Despite this, we may even use the term in the discussion that follows, because it is such convenient shorthand.)

In any discussion of the consequences of restrictions on international trade, it is essential to remember two facts. First, *we pay for imports with exports.* It is true that, in the short run, we can sell off assets or borrow from abroad if we happen to import more goods and services than we export. But we have only a finite amount of assets to sell, and foreigners do not want to wait forever before we pay our bills. Ultimately, our accounts can be settled only if we provide (export) goods and services to the trading partners from whom we purchase (import) goods and services. Trade, after all, involves quid pro quo (literally, something for something). The second point to remember is that *voluntary trade is mutually beneficial to the trading partners.* If we restrict international trade, we reduce those benefits, both for our trading partners and for ourselves. One way these reduced benefits are manifested is in the form of curtailed employment opportunities for workers. In a nutshell, even though tariffs and quotas enhance job opportunities in import-competing industries, they also cost us jobs in export industries; the net effect seems to be reduced employment overall.

What is true for the United States is true for other countries as well: They will only buy our goods if they can market theirs, since they too have to export goods to pay for their imports. Thus any U.S. restrictions on imports to this country—via tariffs, quotas, or other means—ultimately cause a reduction in our exports, because other countries will be unable to pay for our goods. This implies that import restrictions inevitably must decrease the size of our export sector. So imposing trade restrictions to save jobs in import-competing industries has the effect of costing jobs in export industries.

Just as important, import restrictions impose costs on U.S. consumers as a whole. By reducing competition from abroad, quotas, tariffs, and other trade restraints push up the prices of foreign goods and enable U.S. producers to hike their own prices. Perhaps the best documented example of this is found in the automobile industry, where voluntary restrictions on Japanese imports were put in place.

Due in part to the enhanced quality of imported cars, sales of domestically produced automobiles fell from 9 million units in 1978 to an average of 6 million units per year between 1980 and 1982. Profits of U.S. automobile manufacturers plummeted as well, turning into substantial losses for some of them. United States automobile manufacturers and autoworkers' unions demanded protection from import competition. They were joined in their cries by politicians from automobile-producing states. The result was a voluntary agreement entered into by Japanese car companies (the most important competitors of U.S. firms), which restricted U.S. sales of Japanese cars to 1.68 million units per year. This agreement—which amounted to a quota even though it never officially bore that name—began in April 1981 and continued into the 1990s in various forms.

Robert W. Crandall, an economist with the Brookings Institute, has estimated how much this voluntary trade restriction has cost U.S. consumers in terms of higher car prices. According to his estimates, the reduced supply of Japanese cars pushed their prices up by $1500 apiece, measured in 2000 dollars. The higher price of Japanese imports in turn enabled domestic producers to hike their prices an average of $600 per car. The total tab in the first full year of the program was $6.5 billion. Crandall also estimated the number of jobs in automobile-related industries that were saved by the voluntary import restrictions; the total was about 26,000. Dividing $6.5 billion by 26,000 jobs yields a cost to consumers of better than $250,000 *per year* for every job saved in the automobile industry. United States consumers could have saved nearly $2 billion on their car purchases each year if, instead of implicitly agreeing to import restrictions, they had simply given $75,000 to every autoworker whose job was preserved by the voluntary import restraints.

The same types of calculations have been made for other industries. Tariffs in the apparel industry were increased between 1977 and 1981, saving the jobs of about 116,000 U.S. apparel workers at a cost of $45,000 per job each year. At about the same time, the producers of citizens band (CB) radios also managed to get tariffs raised. Approximately 600 workers in the industry kept their jobs as a result but at an annual cost to consumers of over $85,000 per job. The cost of protectionism has been even higher in other industries. Jobs preserved in the glassware industry due to trade restrictions cost $200,000 apiece each year. In the maritime industry, the yearly cost of trade protection is $270,000 per job. In the steel industry, the cost of preserving a job has been estimated at an astounding $750,000 per year. If free trade were permitted, each worker losing a job could be given a cash payment of half that amount each year, and the consumer would still save a lot of money.

Even so, this is not the full story. None of these studies estimating the cost to consumers of saving jobs in import-competing industries have attempted to estimate the ultimate impact of import restrictions on the flow of exports, the number of jobs lost in the export sector, and thus the total number of jobs gained or lost.

When imports to the United States are restricted, our trading partners can afford to buy less of what we produce. The resulting decline in export sales means fewer jobs in exporting industries. And the total reduction in trade leads to fewer jobs for workers such as stevedores (who unload ships) and truck drivers (who carry goods to and from ports). On both counts—the overall cut in trade and the accompanying decline in exports—protectionism leads to job losses that might not be obvious immediately.

Several years ago, Congress tried to pass a domestic content bill for automobiles. In effect, the legislation would have required that cars sold in the United States have a minimum percentage of their components manufactured and assembled in this country. Proponents of the legislation argued that it would have protected 300,000 jobs in the U.S. automobile manufacturing and auto parts supply industries. Yet the legislation's supporters failed to recognize the negative impact of the bill on trade in general and its ultimate impact on U.S. export industries. A U.S. Department of Labor study did recognize these impacts, estimating that the domestic content legislation would actually cost more jobs in trade-related and export industries than it protected in import-competing businesses. Congress ultimately decided not to impose a domestic content requirement for cars sold in the United States.

In principle, trade restrictions are imposed to provide economic help to specific industries and to increase employment in those industries. Ironically, the long-term effects may be just the opposite. Researchers at the World Trade Organization (WTO) examined employment in three industries that have been heavily protected throughout the world—textiles, clothing, and iron and steel. Despite stringent trade protection for these industries, employment actually declined during the period of protection, in some cases dramatically. In textiles employment fell 22 percent in the United States and 46 percent in the European Union. The clothing industry had employment losses ranging from 18 percent in the United States to 56 percent in Sweden. Declines in employment in the iron and steel industry ranged anywhere from 10 percent in Canada to 54 percent in the United States. In short, WTO researchers found that restrictions on free trade were no guarantee against job losses—even in the industries supposedly being protected.

The evidence seems clear: The cost of protecting jobs in the short run is enormous. And in the long run, it appears that jobs cannot be protected, especially if one considers all aspects of protectionism. Free trade is a tough platform on which to run for office. But it looks as if it is the one that will yield the most general benefits if implemented. Of course, this does not mean that politicians will embrace it, and so we end up "saving" jobs at a cost of $750,000 each.

DISCUSSION QUESTIONS

1. Who gains and who loses from import restrictions?

2. What motivates politicians to impose tariffs, quotas, and other trade restrictions?

3. If it would be cheaper to give each steelworker $375,000 per year in cash than impose restrictions on imports of steel, why do we have the import restrictions rather than the cash payments?

4. Most U.S. imports and exports travel through our seaports at some point. How do you predict that members of Congress from coastal states would vote on proposals to restrict international trade? What other information would you want to know in making such a prediction?

GLOSSARY

Cartel: A group of independent industrial corporations, often on an international scale, that agree to restrict trade, to their mutual benefit.

Comparative advantage: The ability to produce goods at a lower cost.

Competition: Rivalry among buyers or sellers of outputs, or among buyers or sellers of inputs.

Cost: Highest-valued (best) foregone alternative; the most valuable option that is sacrificed when a choice is made.

Demand curve: A graphic representation of the demand schedule; a negatively sloped line showing the inverse relationship between the price and the quantity demanded.

Demand schedule: A set of number pairs showing various possible prices and the quantities demanded at each price. This schedule shows the rate of planned purchases per time period at different prices of the good.

E-commerce: Commercial transactions executed over the Internet.

Economic good: Any good or service that is scarce.

Elastic demand: A characteristic of a demand curve in which a given percentage change in price will result in a larger inverse percentage change in quantity demanded. Total revenues and price are inversely related in the elastic portion of the demand curve.

Elasticity: A measure of the responsiveness of one variable to changes in the value of another variable; it equals percentage change in the dependent variable, divided by the percentage change in the independent variable.

Elasticity of demand: The responsiveness of the quantity of a commodity demanded to a change in its price per unit. See also *Price elasticity of demand.*

Elasticity of supply: The responsiveness of the quantity of a commodity supplied to a change in its price per unit. See also *Price elasticity of supply.*

Equilibrium price: The price that clears the market when there is no excess quantity demanded or supplied; the price at which the demand curve intersects the supply curve. Also called *Market-clearing price.*

Externalities: Benefits or costs of an economic activity that spill over to a third party. Pollution is a negative spillover, or externality.

Free good: Any good or service available in larger quantities than desired at a zero price.

Gains from trade: The extent to which individuals, firms, or nations benefit by engaging in exchange.

Inelastic demand: A characteristic of a demand curve in which a given change in price will result in a less-than-proportionate inverse change in the quantity demanded. Total revenue and price are directly related in the inelastic region of the demand curve.

Inflation: A sustained rise in the weighted average of all prices over time.

Law of demand: A law stating that quantity demanded and price are inversely related—more is bought at a lower price, less at a higher price (other things being equal).

Law of supply: A law that states that a direct relationship exists between price and quantity supplied (other things being equal).

Marginal analysis: The analysis of what happens when small changes take place relative to the status quo.

Marginal benefits: The additional (marginal) benefits associated with one more unit of a good or action; the change in total benefits due to the addition of one more unit of production.

Marginal costs: The change in total costs due to a change in one unit of production.

Market clearing price: See **Equilibrium price.**

Market share: The proportion of total sales in an industry accounted for by the sales of a specific firm in that industry.

Market supply: Total quantities of a good offered for sale by suppliers at various prices.

Median age: The age that exactly separates the younger half of the population from the older half.

Merger: The joining together into common ownership of two or more formerly independent companies.

Minimum wage: The lowest hourly wage firms may legally pay their workers.

Models, or theories: Simplified representations of the real world used to make predictions or to better understand the real world.

Monopolist, or **Monopoly:** Literally, a single supplier. More generally, it is a firm that faces a downward-sloping demand curve for its output and therefore can choose the price at which it will sell the good; an example of a *price searcher.*

Monopsonist, or **Monopsony:** Literally, a single buyer. More generally, it is a firm that faces an upward-sloping supply curve for its input and therefore can choose the price at which it will buy the good; an example of a *price searcher.*

Negative externality: A cost, associated with an economic activity, which is paid by third parties. Pollution is a negative externality because, for example, someone other than the driver of an automobile bears part of the cost of the car's exhaust emissions.

Opportunity cost: The highest valued alternative that must be sacrificed to attain something or to satisfy a want.

Per capita income: Total income divided by population.

Perfectly elastic: An infinite value for the ratio of the percentage change in quantity over the percentage change in price, measured along a demand or supply curve; visually, a perfectly elastic curve appears horizontal.

Positive-sum game: A process or setting in which more than one participant gains. Voluntary exchange is said to be a positive-sum game because both parties are simultaneously made better off.

Price elasticity of demand: The percentage change in quantity demanded divided by the percentage change in price. See also *Elasticity of demand.*

Price elasticity of supply: The percentage change in quantity supplied divided by the percentage change in price. See also *Elasticity of supply.*

Price searcher: Literally, a firm that must search for the profit-maximizing price, because it faces a downward-sloping demand curve (if it is a seller) or an upward-sloping supply curve (if it is a buyer); often used as a synonym for *monopoly* or *monopsony*.

Price taker: Any economic agent that takes the market price as given; often used as a synonym for a firm operating in a market characterized by *pure competition.*

Profit: The income generated by selling something for a higher price than was paid for it. In production, the income generated is the difference between total revenues received from consumers who purchase the goods and the total cost of producing those goods.

Property rights: The set of rules specifying how a good may be used and exchanged.

Protectionism: A set of rules designed to protect certain individuals or firms from competition, usually competition from imported goods.

Public goods: Goods with these two characteristics: consumption by one person does not diminish the amount available for others to consume, and it is extremely costly to prevent nonpaying customers from consuming them.

Pure competition: A market structure in which participants individually have no influence over market prices; all act as *price takers.*

Quotas: Limits on the amount of a good or activity; often used in international trade to limit the amount of some foreign good that legally may be imported into a country.

Rate of return: The net benefit, in percentage terms, of engaging in an activity. For example, if the investment of $1.00 yields a gross return of $1.20, the net benefit is $0.20 and the rate of return is equal to ($0.20/$1.00) = 20 percent.

Rent control: A system in which the government tells building owners how much they can charge for rent.

Resource: An input used in the production of desired goods and services.

Scarce good: Any good that commands a positive price.

Scarcity: A state of nature in which resources are limited even though wants are unlimited. Scarcity means that nature does not freely provide as much of everything as people want.

Shortage: A situation in which an excess quantity is demanded or an insufficient quantity is supplied; the difference between the quantity demanded and the quantity supplied at a specific price below the market clearing price.

Social cost: The full cost that society bears when a resource-using action occurs. For example, the social cost of driving a car is equal to all private costs plus any additional cost that other members of society bear (e.g., air pollution and traffic congestion).

Stock: The quantity of something at a point in time. An inventory of goods is a stock. A bank account at a point in time is a stock. Stocks are defined independent of time, although they are assessed at a point in time.

Subsidies: Government payments for the production of specific goods, generally designed to raise the profits of the firms receiving the subsidies and often intended to increase the output of the subsidized goods.

Supply curve: The graphic representation of the supply schedule, which slopes upward (has a positive slope).

Supply schedule: A set of prices and the quantity supplied at each price; a schedule showing the rate of planned production at each relative price for a specified time period.

Surplus: An excess quantity supplied or an insufficient quantity demanded; the difference between the quantity supplied and the quantity demanded at a price above the market clearing price.

Tariffs: Taxes levied on imports.

Trade barriers: Any rules having the effect of reducing the amount of international exchange. *Tariffs* and *quotas* are trade barriers.

Trade-off: A term relating to opportunity cost. In order to get a desired economic good, it is necessary to trade off (give up) some other desired economic good in a situation of scarcity. A trade-off involves making a sacrifice in order to obtain something.

Type I error: An error of commission, such as might arise when an unsafe drug is errantly permitted to be sold.

Type II error: An error of omission, such as might arise if a beneficial drug is errantly prevented from reaching the market.

Vouchers: Government subsidies that can be used only to purchase specified goods, such as education or housing.

Index

The Addison-Wesley Series in Economics